FIGHTING FOR THE FUTURE
Will America Triumph?

Ralph Peters

STACKPOLE
BOOKS

Published by
STACKPOLE BOOKS
5067 Ritter Road
Mechanicsburg, PA 17055
www.stackpolebooks.com

Printed in the United States of America

10 9 8 7 6 5 4 3 2

First Edition

We gratefully acknowledge the cooperation of the following publications for the production of this book: *Parameters*, the U.S. Army War College quarterly, whose editor, John J. Madigan, facilitated our use of those essays that had been printed there; editor Abigail DuBois of *Strategic Review* and Dr. Earl Tilford of the Strategic Studies Institute for the same reason; and the *Army Times* for permission to use Mario Villafuerte's photograph of the author.

Library of Congress Cataloging-in-Publication Data

Peters, Ralph, 1952-
    Fighting for the future : will America triumph? /
    Ralph Peters. — 1st ed.
       p. cm.
    ISBN 0-8117-0651-6 (alk. paper)
    1. War—Forecasting. 2. Military art and science—United States—Forecasting. 3. Twenty-first century—Forecasts. I. Title.
    U21.2.P425 1999
    355.02'01'12—dc21   98-45281
                                                        CIP

Books by Ralph Peters

In memory of
Colonel John J. Madigan III
United States Army, Retired
1936–1999
Patriot, Scholar, Gentleman

History is a bath of blood.
—William James

Contents

The Background of This Book

The notion that the pen is mightier than the sword is a fantasy. Try waving a book at the man who comes after you with a machete or a gun. Yet the pen can inform the sword. That is the aim of these essays.

An unusual military career and a compulsion to keep moving took me to more than forty countries. I served in Cold War Europe as an empire failed. While the Soviet Union lay dying, I explored its guts. I listened to butchers' lies over tea in the offices of Moscow's security services and saw the suffering of remote wars. Other assignments took me to the Pentagon and the Executive Office of the President, to the Andean Ridge, to Southeast Asia, and to America's broken cities. Personal fascination drew me to the eastern Mediterranean world again and again, and luck brought me to the banks of the Indus. I saw the world through my own eyes, not refracted by libraries. In these travels, official and not, it became clear to me that our government's understanding of the world does not extend much beyond our embassy grounds and hotel lobbies.

My sector of our government was the U.S. Army. I enlisted as a private after the Army had been broken by Vietnam. I became an officer through the back door. I loved the Army passionately and served in it for over two decades before the fire faded from the romance. I am loyal to it still, much as one might care for an old lover felled by drink and bad decisions. For much of my career, the Army was dynamic, creative, and honest. *Sic transit veritas mundi,* to twist a cliché. Increasingly, though, I saw our military avoiding hard thought and difficult decisions, hypnotizing itself with empty mantras. After Vietnam, anger had saved the Army. A generation of bloodied crusaders rebuilt the force and unleashed it in Desert Storm. I watched those heroes from the trenches with awe. And now they are gone. Today, I see apathy and confusion and mediocrity. We still have the greatest army in the world, but it is greatness by legacy.

Two misfortunes struck our military during my career. First, the Soviet system collapsed, robbing us of a cherished, vivid enemy. Second, the U.S. armed forces performed magnificently in and above the deserts of Mesopotamia, convincing a generation of leaders that perfection had been attained. Like the Israelis, we allowed the ineptitude of a specific adversary to convince us of our general superiority. In the midst of the most dynamic period of change in history, our military leaders chose stasis veiled by massive and wasteful procurement.

Our Army, and our military, is inherently conservative. It needs to be pulled along by the rest of government and by society. On the eve of our entry into the Second World War, as the German *Blitzkrieg* ravished Europe, the Army's proudest unit was a horse cavalry division. Had war not forced change upon us, we would have preserved that division into the 1960s, at least. Instead of an interstate highway system, we would have gotten an interstate bridle path.

We live in the most unsettled, spiritually turbulent age in history, a period of multiple and layered revolutions. In the realms of failure—they are and will be legion—hatred is currency, and violence language. Ours is a world we wish to change, but do not understand. As I roamed the globe, I saw a fundamental asymmetry between the kind of military force we prized and the sort we would need. I also became convinced that traditional boundaries between the military, economic, civil, and cultural spheres were crumbling. Although the ultimate business of our military will always be to make war, I sensed that we would become involved in many activities that did not match our traditions, and that officers would need to learn to see more broadly, to act more acutely, and to acquire different skills. Officers will always need the killer instinct. But today, they also need the discipline of a saint, the insight of an anthropologist, and the acrobat's sense of balance.

Perhaps there is too much of the old Welsh Dissenter in my blood, but I believed that I saw the world with greater clarity than many of my peers, and the need grew in me to testify to my vision. So I wrote, with the miner's tenacity that was my inheritance.

The 1980s were a golden age of military thought and debate in our country. In the 1990s, I profited from that legacy. *Parameters,* the journal of the U.S. Army War College, encouraged independent thought and critical analysis. With the decline of the old Russian-language monthly *Military Thought, Parameters* had become the world's preeminent periodical for military-strategic theory. Successive editors pushed beyond the traditional boundaries of "military" subjects. It is a mark of the courage of those editors (retired Colonels Lloyd Matthews and John Madigan) that they would print the work of an officer who questioned the omniscience of the Army's leadership—and had fun doing it.

The essays in this book found more success than any of us expected. They were widely reprinted, shamelessly plagiarized, and productively looted. A range of military schools and universities used them in their curricula, and they gained an international following. The business community, too, found the strategic implications of interest. Most importantly, officers actually read them. The ideas inspired change. I hope that they have served a good purpose and that they have done no harm.

From the beginning, I had decided to take a multiavenue approach in my personal offensive. I wrote these "serious" essays for a core audience. Simultaneously, however, I wrote page-turner novels that humanized strategic themes, for I have never deluded myself that decision makers or the public could be brought to theoretical writings en masse (the greatest fantasy of twentieth-century revolutionaries was that a working man would go home after a hard day and read Marx). It was an effort on a broad front and, frankly, a war of attrition, because that is how you change organizations. Maneuver warfare is for the battlefield, not bureaucracies. You must pound bureaucracies and not stop. You have to grind them down.

The essays led to lectures, Internet stalkings, and a notoriety that drew attacks from left and right. They were controversial when published, although not all appear so now. Yesterday's sensation is today's commonplace. This is, I think, the hallmark of influence.

But no one article, nor any ten, will change our mammoth defense establishment. Rather, you must write and work for a cumulative effect. It is your converts—often unwitting—who further the cause of change and preach it on their missionary journeys through their careers.

Strategy is theology with the hope left out. It is about the death of some and the survival of others, and its greatest constructions break on the rock of the world. No individual has all the essential questions, let alone useful answers to them. Each pilgrim on the long road of change must be content to make his or her contribution to the collective effort and to taste disappointment. Only that long—theological—view lends at least an illusion of worth to our efforts. Preachers come and go, but the congregation remains.

So here are my essays, written over six years with passion, love, and sometimes despair. They are ultimately small, as is the work of every man. The pen is not mightier than the sword, but an able pen can help design a better sword. That has been my enduring goal.

Ultimately, I have a simple view of history and of the future. I see mankind as forever torn between the Sermon on the Mount and the story of Cain and Abel. We may long for the peaceable kingdom, but Cain will always be with us. We will need good soldiers to deal with him.

The book you hold in your hands is the result of one soldier doing the best that he could.

The Culture of Future Conflict

The computer will not replace the book, and postmodern forms of conflict will not fully replace conventional war. We will, however, experience a bewildering expansion of the varieties of collective and factional violence. The computer expands our possibilities and alters methods of working and organizing. So, too, the worldwide crisis in systems of social organization and belief broadens the range of challenges to global, regional, and local order. States and military establishments that restrict their preparations, initiatives, and responses to traditional patterns will pay for their fear of the future in blood, money, and quality of life.

Although man and his failings will remain at the center of war and conflict, a unique combination of factors will precipitate and shape events. At least into the seventeenth century, Western man believed that planetary and stellar conjunctions were responsible for disasters on the earth. Today, we face a constellation of crises much closer to home with profound strategic and military implications. The warning comet is already with us as we approach a dark new century.

Future wars and violent conflicts will be shaped by the inabilities of governments to function as effective systems of resource distribution and control, and by the failure of entire cultures to compete in the postmodern age. The worldwide polarization of wealth, afflicting continents and countries, as well as individuals in all countries, will prove insurmountable, and social divisions will spark various forms of class warfare more brutal than anything imagined by Karl Marx. Poststate organizations, from criminal empires to the internationalizing media, will rupture the integrity of the nation-state. Niche technologies, such as postmodern means of information manipulation and dissemination, will provoke at least as often as they produce and will become powerful tools of conflict. Basic resources will prove inadequate for populations exploding beyond natural limits, and we may discover truths about ourselves that we do not wish to know. In the end, the greatest challenge may be to our moral order.

The greatest challenge may be to our moral order.

The incompetence of the state has been demonstrated along fault lines from the former Yugoslavia and desperate North Korea to Congo/Zaire and Liberia. The "state" as we revere it is a cultural growth and must develop organically— where it has been grafted it rarely takes. The Euro-American and East Asian state's civility as well as its authority rely on expanding wealth, on a perceived community of interests that allows public compromise or acquiescence, and on individual and collective senses of responsibility. In many of the "states" that presently hold seats in the United Nations, per capita wealth is declining, there is no community of interests, nor is there an individual sense of responsibility for the common good. Even in Western states, the vital sense of generalized responsibility is deteriorating as interest groups promote factionalization and citizen expectations grow excessive and wantonly selfish.

In many "accidental states" shaped hastily in the recession of empire, state structures survived only through their ability to apply internal violence. Today, even these oppressive construct-states are breaking down as burgeoning populations make state-sponsored violence against their own citizens statistically ineffectual. Simultaneously, thanks largely to the temptress Media, worldwide citizen expectations of government have wildly surpassed the abilities of government to deliver (the gray area between possibilities and needs/wants is the age-old breeding ground of organized crime and political radicalism). This is true of the United States and of Algeria. Fortunately for us in the United States, our government's ability to deliver generally exceeds requirements, if not expectations. In Algeria, government shortcomings have led to a cultural struggle that has engulfed the state and threatens to destroy it.

Cultural failure has many historical precedents, from the collapse of the Hittite empire to the destruction of the Aztecs, but there has never before been a time when a single dominant culture and its imitators have threatened to overwhelm every other major culture on earth. Even in the great age of European empire, most of the conquered peoples remained free to practice their own religions and lifestyles, blissfully unaware of a seductive alternative model. Today, thanks to the distribution of addictively Western films, videos, television, and radio to even the most obscure and hopeless backwaters, there is an unprecedented worldwide awareness of relative physical and cultural poverty within non-Western cultures. Western models of behavior and possession—often misunderstood—create crises of identity and raise appetites that local environments cannot sate. Increasingly, we live in a world where the Flintstones meet the Jetsons—and the Flintstones don't much like it. When they try to imitate our performance, they fail, except in the case of gifted individuals. When they try to secede from the West, they fail again. In the end, there is only rage.

There has never before been a time when a single dominant culture and its imitators have threatened to overwhelm every other major culture on earth.

Wealth polarization is worsening after a century of limited progress toward equalization. The United States and a few other adept nation-states have entered a wealth-generation cycle for which there is no predictable end, despite intermittent trade squabbles and recessions. But the nature of postmodern competition is such that membership in this club is closing. Although some disciplined, culturally predisposed states may eventually join the rich West-plus, they will be exceptions. The value of manual and mass labor is plunging in a world of surplus population, while the skills necessary for successful economies and desirable jobs increasingly rely on the total environment in which the individual lives and learns, from infancy forward. In the past, fortunate individuals could jump from premodern to modern. But the gap between premodern and postmodern is too great to be crossed in a single leap. The economically vibrant jobs of the next century will demand "transcendent literacy": the second-nature ability to read, write, think abstractly, and manipulate information electronically. This fateful shift is already creating painful dislocations in our own country and threatens to create an expanded and irredeemable underclass. Its effect on the non-Western world will be to condemn states, peoples, and even continents to enduring poverty.

Social division is the obvious result of the polarization of wealth. Although most of the world's population has always been condemned to poverty, a combination of religious assurance, ignorance of how well others lived, and hope for a better future more often than not curbed man's natural rage at wealth discrepancies. Now the slum dwellers of Lagos are on to the lifestyles of the rich and famous, while hopes of prosperity even for a future generation dwindle. In the West-plus, this bifurcation into skilled and well-off versus unskilled and poor has created archipelagoes of failure in a sea of success. The rest of the world contains only fragile archipelagoes of success in vast, increasingly stormy seas of failure. Occasionally, the failures attack us at home, staging events, such as the World Trade Center bombing, that are as spectacular as they are statistically ineffective. More often, these unmoderns take out their inchoate anger on the nearest targets—rival clans or tribes, citizens of minority religions or ethnicities, or their own crumbling governments. Intermittently, these local rages will aggrieve our extraterritorial welfare—primarily our economic interests—and we will need to intervene. In the twentieth century, the great wars were between ambitious winner-states. In the coming century, the routine conflicts to which we will be party will pit those same winner-states, now reconciled, against vast "loser" populations in failed states and regions.

The rise of the anti-state in various forms has been and will be the result of the failure of governments to cater to basic needs and to satisfy expanding desires. The anti-state can take many forms, from media conglomerates that determine what the world should know, through much-maligned peace-preferring multinational corporations, to webs of criminality expanding across oceans, enterprise disciplines, and cultures. In the world of the anti-state, international criminals often cooperate more effectively and creatively than do states. Criminal enterprise mirrors legitimate enterprise in its focus on secure profits, but its "integrity" exceeds that of the greatest multinationals because the criminal anti-state has a galvanizing enemy: the state fighting for its life. It is in the adaptive nature of the postmodern anti-state that it can develop a symbiotic relationship even with a formal government it strategically penetrates, as criminal anti-state webs have done in Russia, Nigeria, Mexico, and numerous less-spectacular examples.

Anti-states also take the forms of premodern structures, such as tribal or religious identifications. At the high end of development we are witnessing the birth of new "tribes" based on skills, wealth, and cultural preferences. As with the old, enduring tribes, the geographic domain of these new communities rarely matches the contours of existing state borders.

We are entering an era of multidimensional, interpenetrating structures of social control, wealth allocation, and even allegiance. The decline of the state, real or relative, accelerates under *knowledge assault,* as new structures of knowing outpace the ability of traditional governments to process and respond to information. The modern age was the age of mass efficiencies. The postmodern age is the age of mass inefficiencies, wherein bigness equals clumsiness and lethargy. Ours is increasingly an age of neoanarchic "cellular" accomplishment that, at its best, gives us enhanced microchips and, at its worst, turns the world's cities into criminal harbors. Reduced to the fundamentals, we face a conflict between blood ties and knowledge ties. Ours is a world whose constituents may lurch backward as well as forward, but in which nothing can remain unchanged.

Decisive technologies, from the birth control pill to the computer, have exploded traditional forms of organization, behavior, and belief in our lifetimes. Technology can lead to enhanced environmental mastery—but it can also lead to fatal dependencies. The best example of this pits the computer against the television. A skilled computer user is an active "techno-doer." Unless he or she is particularly creative, this computerist is the postmodern blue-collar worker, the new machinist. This computerist adds value in the classic sense enshrined by Marx, Keynes, and Schumpeter. On the other hand, the passive television viewer, especially one possessing a VCR, confuses us because we imagine that he or she is mastering technology. On the contrary, the technology is mastering the human. The passive "techno-user" adds no value and may even lose operative abilities and initiative. This is not an attack on television in general, which can be a powerful tool for the dissemination of information; rather, it is a warning that technology consumers do not necessarily become technologically capable. *A society must produce techno-doers,* and all technologies, active and passive, must find a healthy integrative level. Otherwise, the force of technology is destructive, if deceptively comforting in its amusement value. Dangerous for segments of our own society, this addictive passivity can be fatal to noncompetitive cultures.

Rich issues also arise out of our attempts to redefine "military technology" in the postmodern age, but there is one respect in which all relevant branches of Westernness, from the military through business, are alike. Increasingly, we take our entire environment with us when we go. From techno-gypsies working their laptops in jungle backwaters to the military that fought Desert Storm, we are learning to insulate ourselves as never before from the inefficiencies of the non-West. This is the first, unavoidable step toward an enclavement of our civilization that excludes the noncompetitive.

Resource scarcity will be a direct cause of confrontation, conflict, and war. The struggle to maintain access to critical resources will spark local and regional conflicts that will evolve into the most frequent conventional wars of the next century. Today, the notion of resource wars leads the Westerner to think immediately of oil, but water will be the fundamental need of some states, anti-states, and peoples. We envision a need to preserve rain forests, but expanding populations will increasingly create regional shortages of food—especially when nature turns fickle. We are entering the century of "not enough," and we will bleed for things we once could buy.

Gross overpopulaton will destroy fragile possibilities for progress in much of the non-Western world, and much of this problem is the West's fault. Our well-intentioned introduction of relatively crude concepts of sanitation and disease control, combined with our determination to respond generously to local famines, has allowed populations to explode. Changes in public health so small a Westerner would not notice them can have spectacular effects in underdeveloped societies. For instance, reductions in infant mortality can occur swiftly, but it takes generations for societies to adjust to the value-challenging concept of family planning—and some refuse to adjust. Thus, populations increase geometrically as behavior lags technology. These population increases lead to greater urbanization, as the countryside and traditional structures cannot support the additional surviving offspring and the city appears to offer economic opportunity and a more attractive lifestyle. But few economies outside of the West-plus can create jobs as quickly as they are creating job seekers. Even rates of economic growth that sound remarkable leave Third World countries with ever-greater unemployed and underemployed masses. The result is an even further breakdown of traditional structures and values. In the end, the only outlet for a lifetime's frustration is violence.

Now and future plagues are the present nightmares of choice on the best-seller lists and movie screens of the United States. The general scenario has a new disease exploding out of its previously isolated lair in the Third World and hopping a flight to Gringoland, where it behaves with the random destructiveness of an inner-city teenager. Certainly, this is a plausible scenario, and one against which we must guard. But the real threat to this planet's future may be just the opposite: disease is one of nature's many corrective mechanisms. *Our battle against disease may prove too successful,* resulting in populations that the earth's resources cannot sustain and precipitating literally endless human misery and conflict. Whereas the pandemics of the past were tragic for countless individuals, they were only rarely tragic for societies or cultures—and never for mankind as a whole. Indeed, epidemic disease may have been our dark, unrecognized friend, not only as a population regulator but also as a catalyst for dynamic change. Certainly, there has never been a single disease, not even the oft-cited Black Death, that seriously threatened to wipe out mankind—only human beings know how to do that.

So what does it all mean? There will be fewer classic wars but more violence. While conventional war will remain the means of last resort to resolve interstate confrontations, the majority of conflicts will be asymmetrical, with a state or coalition of states only one of the possible participants. The rise of nonstate threats is a tremendous problem for Western governments and militaries, because we are legally and behaviorally prepared to fight only other legal-basis states—mirror images of ourselves—at a time when state power and substance are declining worldwide.

"Survivalists" in North America have it exactly wrong. While they fear a metastasizing, increasingly intrusive, globalizing state, the world is fracturing, and our own government has less control over the behavior of its citizens than at any time during the twentieth century. *The survivalists fear excessive lawfulness, when the problem is exploding lawlessness*—or the inability to enforce existing laws. While our state occasionally falters, foreign states are collapsing, and we face constituencies of the damned, of the hopeless, from whose midst arise warrior classes for whom peace is the least rewarding human condition. As we in the West enter the postmodern age, much of the non-West (starting at the borders of the former Yugoslavia) looks like the Trojan War with machine guns and, perhaps eventually, with nuclear weapons.

What will future conflicts look like? Traditional forms of warfare will remain, with the Middle East and the Asian landmass as their primary cockpit, but these conventional wars will be supplemented with new and hybrid forms of conflict. *Civil wars*—usually distinctly uncivil in their conduct—are a growth industry, as cultures and societies attempt to resolve their threatened, globally incompetent identities. Although these civil wars will intermittently threaten Western interests, rule-bound military interventions will not be able to bring them to closure. Today, many human societies are cultural ecosystems striving to regain equilibrium, often through gruesome civil wars. The introduction of powerful foreign elements only further upsets the equilibrium and guarantees exaggerated bloodshed after the intervening power has withdrawn.

Dying states will resort to violence against their own populations in last-gasp efforts to maintain power, spawning expanded *insurgencies*. Elsewhere, state inefficiencies and the lack of ethnic or cultural harmony will spark revolts and terrorism. Massive criminal insurgencies are a new method of challenging the state through violence. In Southeast Asia's Golden Triangle and in the Andean Ridge, druglord insurgencies moved from defying laws to denying great tracts of territory to the state. In Russia, a confluence between organized crime and government in lucrative spheres constitutes a quiet criminal coup. Nigerian criminality looks to exceed oil income as the primary revenue of the state in the future. In the past, insurgencies were easy to recognize—the rebels marched on the presidential palace. Today, some of the most threatening criminal insurgencies in the non-West will be conducted by officials already *inside* the presidential palace. We cannot respond to such top-down insurgencies under international codes of law designed for a world run by Woodrow Wilsons.

Aftermath instability is already a pernicious problem and will worsen. In the wake of high-level agreements to resolve conflicts, most broken states or territories cannot reabsorb the human detritus left behind by waves of violence. With a previously inadequate infrastructure further degraded by conflict, even individuals who desire to live in peace often cannot find shelter or adequate food, much less employment. For those who have become habituated to violence and its quick rewards, postconflict societies often have nothing to offer that can wean these warriors back to constructive patterns of behavior. As populations expand and hatreds deepen, we will find that, although a swift, determined military intervention may bring a formal end to some conflicts, informal conflict will persist indefinitely, destroying any hopes for local societal healing.

Intercultural struggles, with their unbridled savagery, are the great nightmare of the next century.

Intercultural struggles, with their unbridled savagery, are the great nightmare of the next century, and a great deal has been written about them, either warning of the "Clash of Civilizations" à la Huntington or, in outraged, well-intentioned responses, assuring us that everybody will get along just fine if the West sends money. While we may dread the moral and practical issues that intercultural competition poses, this struggle is already upon us, with parties hostile to the West forcing the issue to the extent of their still-limited competencies. If present conflicts evolve toward open warfare, this could be the defining struggle of the next century—as ideological competition was for the twentieth century. The question is whether we can manage such conflicts with nonmilitary means or whether they will deepen and spread until they require a general military response. At present, it appears likely that our military will find itself drawn into intercultural struggles in future decades—if only because it will be impossible to appease challengers bent on supplanting us, punishing us, or destroying us. If there is a single power the West underestimates, it is the power of collective hatred.

If there is a single power the West underestimates, it is the power of collective hatred.

Cataclysm response will continue to demand military participation. Traditional natural disasters, short of world plagues, are ultimately manageable and do not fatally divert military resources. Man-made cataclysms are another matter. Even peacekeeping is a form of cataclysm response—and a very expensive one. Further, the proliferation and terrible condition of nuclear facilities in much of the Northern Hemisphere make Chernobyl look like a precedent rather than an anomaly. We also will see a growing cross-fertilization between cataclysm and conflict, with one feeding on or aggravating the other. Whereas past wars often spread famine or plague in their wakes, we may be entering a period of renewed spoils taking or even wars of annihilation. From Kuwait to Rwanda, the comfortable modern boundaries between man-made and natural disasters have already begun to break down in postmodern confusion.

The strategic military implications are clear—at least in part. But those implications can be more easily discussed than practically addressed. First, we will see an *expeditionary West,* condemned to protect its distant interests. Given our finite resources, we will have to weigh national interests against human interests, asking ourselves whether to intervene for humanitarian reasons and whether our national interests may be contrary to non-Western human interests. We are not going to get off easily in the conscience department. We often will have to redefine victory in an era of unwinnable wars and conflicts. Sometimes the dilemma will be whether there is an advantage to an intervention that only delays resolution. We may have to recast traditional military roles when faced with criminal insurgencies or foreign corruption so wildly out of control it threatens our national interests. We will face a dangerous temptation to seek purely technological responses to behavioral challenges—especially given the expense of standing forces. Our cultural strong suit is the ability to balance and integrate the technological with the human, and we must continue to stress getting that balance right. We must beware of wonder weapons that offer no significant advantage in a changing world.

There are practical military considerations, as well. We will fight men who do not look, think, or act like us, and this can lead to a dangerous dehumanizing of the enemy, just as it will make it more difficult for us to understand him. We will fight in cities, and this brutal, casualty-prone, dirty kind of combat will negate many of our technological advantages while it strains our physical and moral resources. Technology will continue to pile up new wonders, but we will find that there are sharp limits to what technology can add to our effectiveness in asymmetrical conflicts. The quality of leaders and soldiers will become even more important as we fight in smaller increments, whether on an "empty" postmodern battlefield or in the overcrowded, dysfunctional cities of failing states. We will encounter unprecedented densities of noncombatants stranded in the maelstrom of urban combat. And we will try, whenever possible, to cocoon our forces in "movable fortresses"—not classic fortresses with physical walls but transferred environments with electronic, missile, and fire barriers, antiseptic support environments, and impenetrable information structures. This will work best in conventional warfare, but our efficacy in setting the terms of involvement will deteriorate the farther down the scale of organized conflict we must descend. No matter how hard we try to take our world with us, we will still find that we sometimes must fight the enemy on his ground, by his rules. This is the hardest form of combat for the United States, because our own rules cripple us and, at worst, kill us.

The new century will bring new weapons, and some of those weapons will bring moral dilemmas. For example, suppose that discoveries in fields as seemingly diverse as evolutionary biology, neurology, complexity studies, advanced sonics, computerization, and communications allowed us to create a "broadcast weapon" that could permanently alter human behavior without causing physical harm. We would immediately face protests from concerned parties to whom it would, paradoxically, be more humane to kill an enemy than to interfere with his or her free will.

Other new weapons will require the military to expand its skill range, and leader-to-led ratios will need to be increased in favor of low-level leaders, because of the new skills required by technological advances and because of the compartmentalization effect of urban combat and the dispersion of the conventional battlefield. The oldest forms of warfare, such as in-close individual combat, will coexist with over-the-horizon cyberspace

attacks. And again and again, we will face well-intentioned inter-
locutors who insist that, since the military never did that, it
shouldn't be allowed to do it now. An enduring tension
between expanding missions and traditional strictures will ham-
per military operations. We will face repeated situations in
which we are asked to send our soldiers into conflicts for which
they have been physically well trained but in which the rules we
impose on them leave them practically defenseless. We must
learn as a country to identify that which we truly need to
achieve, and then to assess honestly the necessary means of getting to that achievement. It is the duty of our military leadership to inform that debate.

What will our twenty-first-century world look like? For the
successful, it will be an age of nontraditional empires. The
United States in particular, and the West in general, currently
possesses a cultural and business empire that touches all parts
of the globe. It is far more efficient and rewarding than any
previous form of empire has been. The Russian Federation is
trying to build an empire on the cheap, in a less benign form,
in which regional political, military, economic, and resource
hegemony takes the place of large armies of occupation, waves
of colonization, and expensive local administrations. Traditional colonies have disappeared not because of liberation ideology but because they were ultimately unprofitable and too
difficult to manage. The new empire largely manages itself.

As noncompetitive regions decline, wealth enclaves will
emerge, primarily in the West-plus. The "colonies" of the
future will be controlled economically and "medially," not
politically, and will focus on resources and markets. The political and then the military arms of West-plus governments will
become involved only when business encounters disadvanta-

geous illegal behaviors or violence—today, the flag follows trade. West-plus governments will police physical and digital "safe corridors" for resource extraction, general trade, and information ranching, but in failed countries and continents, the West-plus will be represented primarily by postmodern traders.

The great dangers that could spark broad conventional wars will be resource competition and cultural confrontations—or a volatile combination of both, which could arise, for instance, in the Persian Gulf–Caspian Sea macroregion. Worldwide social bifurcation will lead increasingly to a triage approach to diplomacy, aid, and interventions, and a sobered West will prove necessarily selective in its military deployments, concentrating on financial interests and lifestyle protection.

By the middle of the next century, if not before, the overarching mission of our military will be the preservation of our quality of life.

After the Revolution

The latest "revolution in military affairs" occurred in the 1980s. It is over now. A new paradigm prevails. There will be no end to the technological miracles that alter the geometries of conventional battlefields and theaters while reshaping budgets and forces. But machines, no matter how magnificent, do not of themselves constitute a revolution. True revolutions happen, above all, in the minds of men. By that measure, the military has undergone a profound and irreversible revolution. The average officer today perceives the temporal, spatial, and mechanical dimensions of warfare in a radically different manner than did his predecessor of twenty years ago. The changes have been internalized to such a degree that we must pause and think about them in order to recognize how far we have come in a breathtakingly short period.

Anyone who doubts that we have entered a postrevolutionary order need only consider the popularity of seminars and publications devoted to the Revolution in Military Affairs, or RMA—irrefutable indicators that any truly revolutionary activity is over. The drag-on debates about whether there has been or is an RMA, what it portends, and how it differs from the "military-technical revolution" are frivolous and irrelevant. The endless symposiums, studies, and articles are popular because they promise a new home to those intellectually dispossessed by the end of the Cold War. Thinking about the manageable secondary problem of the military application of technology in the future saves us from having to think meaningfully about the brutal, intractable issues immediately confronting our nation, our allies, and our interests.

Revolutions happen, above all, in the minds of men.

Our national security problems have more to do with innovative behaviors than with military-technological competition. The advent of criminal and warlord parastates is a far more urgent challenge than funding the B-2 bomber boys' club. We are witnessing multiple simultaneous revolutions—and devolutions—in worldwide social and governmental structures, and millennia-old patterns of human organization are collapsing. Amid galaxies of shining technologies there is a struggle to redefine human meaning. Technology is changing how man knows, and the resulting dislocations are culturally cataclysmic. Half the world is looking for God anew, and the other half is behaving as though no god exists. The RMA is a subset of a subset in the hierarchy of contemporary revolutions. By elevating the now-historical issue of the RMA to the top of our military agenda, we have fallen into the old American trap of seeking technological solutions to human problems, of so immersing ourselves in questions of form that we overlook fundamental issues of function.

We in the Department of Defense—and even more so those in the Department of State—live in the nineteenth century philosophically. Our understanding of our respective roles and missions is a vestige of a fading order. We face a world in which the nineteenth-century manner of organizing and applying the power of the state is of marginal relevance. Far from the conventionally armed and recognizably structured forces our analysts stretch to imagine as future opponents, we confront, *today,* creatively organized enemies employing behaviors and technologies ranging from those of the Stone Age to those at the imagination's edge. If we do not stop ducking behind a combination of obsolescent reservations about what militaries do or do not do and the wizardly technologies we buy to disguise our fear of the future, our post-RMA military may prove to be the most expensive white elephant in the history of mankind.

This is not an argument against technology, nor against robust conventional forces, which we will need as long as murderers realize that there is strength in numbers. It is, rather, a plea for putting the horse before the cart, for stepping back and conducting the painful, rigorous analysis necessary to employ technology relevantly and to shape a force to fit the times, for asking basic questions about our identity and purpose.

Only one potential new weapons complex appears genuinely vital to our national security for the budgetary future: multilevel ballistic missile defenses, critical because of the proliferation of missile and nuclear technologies. If the U.S. armed forces were otherwise to execute a ten-year moratorium on the fielding of all new weapons systems, concentrating instead on research and development; continued experimentation; the improvement of support systems, training, and readiness; and, above all, human factors, would our nation's security be seriously endangered, or would it be enhanced?

Technologically, we are riding a change wave that threatens to make present and pending technologies rapidly obsolete. New weapons bought today may provide ten or so years of superiority—which we already have anyway—but as general research accelerates, purchases delayed until after the turn of the century may offer a full generation or more of advantage, since competitors will be less able to rise to the infrastructural requirements of the hyperadvanced technologies that will become available. In the meantime, the real threats we face imply a new lease on life for skilled infantry and an enduring need for special operations forces. We need to continue to stress transport and communications. Our intelligence networks need to regain a tactile human sense and to exploit information technologies without becoming enslaved by them. In most of our recent deployments, no one weapon system, no matter how expensive and technologically mature, has been as valuable as a single culturally competent foreign area officer.

There is not one compelling reason to buy a single additional bomber, fighter, submarine, or tank today, save the preservation of the industrial base. Yet even that is a dubious cause; when tens of billions of dollars are involved, even the most skeptical hawk is apt to be amazed at how quickly the private sector can regenerate a needed production capability. If legislators wish to continue workfare programs for defense workers, let us at least be honest about it and not pretend to the American people that their security depends on systems in search of a mission when the real issue is whether we understand the world system decomposing around us.

At present, we are preparing for the war we want to fight someday, not for the conflicts we cannot avoid.

Our understanding of and approach to international relations and the use of the military are based on an assumption of the ubiquity of the nation-state. We play by rules, some encoded in our own laws or in international laws and customs, others matters of habit that have so long endured that they have acquired totemic power in our collective consciousness. When other world actors play by our rules, we triumph. Increasingly, however, the world doesn't give a damn about our laws, customs, or table manners.

We are preparing for the war we want to fight . . .
not for the conflicts we cannot avoid.

In much of the world, the nation-state model we cherish is declining in relevance and functionality. From Colombia to Russia, traditional structures of government coexist nervously with emerging systems of resource allocation and human organization, from techno-capable crime networks to the machete-swinging clans of warlords, from Russia's neofeudal oligarchy through economic migrations to the reemergence of the city-state in places such as Bogotá, Sarajevo, and Kabul. The future of China may resemble that of classical Greece, with its rival cities, blood feuds, and a contest of militarism with commerce.

Increasingly, in multiple spheres of human activity, postformal webs of control operate transnationally, ignoring borders we still pretend are sacrosanct. What does sovereignty mean to a drug cartel, except that *narcotraficantes* cannot be pursued across an invisible frontier? Our Department of State is a magnificent

tool for dealing with symmetrically structured, like-minded entities—but what has it accomplished in Somalia? In Bosnia
(besides guaranteeing the gains of ethnic cleansers)? In Africa's
ruptured Gold Coast territories?

Again and again, we find that hard-won treaties mean nothing because we negotiated them with governments that have
only nominal authority while the true sources of local power are
asymmetrical to our own. We shake hands with warlords, smil-
ing for the length of a photo opportunity, only to discover, in
the words of that master of practical philosophy Samuel Gold-
wyn, that "an oral contract isn't worth the paper it's printed
on." We are becoming word-people, and we face deed-people,
and we don't even have an adequate vocabulary to describe
them. Imprisoned by the pathetically outdated terminology of
diplomacy and international relations, we find that we cannot
accurately describe what is happening, and therefore we cannot
think it. We are speaking Latin in the computer age.

The borders we see on maps increasingly do not exist on
the ground. Further, our emerging opponents could not care
less about the way we divide responsibilities among diplomats,
lawyers, soldiers, and cops—except when they can exploit
those divisions. Our opponents, crime chiefs and tribal chiefs
alike, operate in environments of tremendous moral and practical freedom, and increasingly they assimilate relevant technologies much more swiftly than can the regulation-bound,
labor-intensive bureaucracies of struggling nation-states. The
government of Colombia affects Colombia—when it affects
anything at all. Colombian drug cartels have a powerful effect
on much of the developed world. But diplomatic practice
demands that we deal only with and through the government
in Bogotá.

The imaginary sanctity of the nation-state tyrannizes our behavior, while terrorists, drug traffickers, resource pirates, and post-Soviet crime networks dance across continents and oceans. The fluidity with which the most sophisticated of our opponents range internationally resembles the flow of dollars in the international financial system. We move like sacks of cement. Where the opponents of our order find opportunities, we encounter barriers. We negotiate status-of-forces agreements. The bad guys just get on a plane and go.

Criminal organizations, to stress only one of the growing and largely ignored threats to our national security, increasingly have more power than do failing states. We refuse to face the consequences, insisting that all crime is a "law-enforcement problem." But the veil of illusion is disintegrating, no matter how desperately we may try to patch it up. Latin America's problems are already a cliché. Kurdish insurrections run on heroin receipts from Berlin and Stockholm. In Africa and post-Soviet Eurasia, it is impossible to construct a firebreak between government and organized crime. In Russia, the military is often for rent when it is not for sale. Historically, organized crime has inhabited the gap between people's needs and expectations and their government's ability to fulfill them. Today, with the efficacy of formal government in worldwide decline, criminal organizations are becoming new forms of government (for want of a new and better word), often on a local level, but increasingly on a national scale. While historians may argue that some forms of government have long manifested criminal behaviors, from feudal Europe to postcolonial Africa, a key difference is that old-model "criminal" governments were almost invariably inward looking. Today's new model of criminal government has regional, even worldwide, ambitions.

This has powerful implications for statecraft and military activities even where the United States is not actively engaged. Over the past few decades, a focus of our diplomacy and military assistance has been to help Third World militaries evolve toward the twentieth-century U.S. model of civil-military relations and task allocation, in which the military looks outward and law-enforcement agencies do the domestic chores. After years of "progress," this model is breaking down everywhere. Criminal, terrorist, or other armed nonstate organizations have grown too powerful and adept—in extreme cases, we even see the emergence of criminal enterprise armies (CEAs). CEAs may not have the organization and hitting power of CENTCOM, but they are increasingly more than a match for underpaid, undertrained, underequipped Third World cops—or even for regional militaries. From Colombia to Anatolia, traditional governments are fighting for their lives against border-hopping, criminally funded, increasingly well-equipped CEAs that know how to exploit Western tools, from human rights activists through banks and lawyers to the media. We attack our allies and clients for using military means to fight back: the U.S. government formally deplores the use of military means in almost any form to enforce domestic stability. Yet domestic employment of our National Guard in countercrime operations appears an inevitable part of our own future, at least on our borders and in extreme urban environments (where our forces have already accumulated a dismaying amount of experience).

Organized crime is only one of the dirty fingers clawing at our future. Others range from hatreds based on hereditary identifications, to the forlorn, violent attempts of overwhelmed cultures to detach themselves from Western influences, to resource wars. As our own society continues to fracture between those who can adapt to postmodernity and those who cannot, an archipelago of failure is emerging within the United States, posing problems so intractable and concentrated that traditional law enforcement may prove unable to contain them. Still, the most frequent "battlefields" for our military in the looming wars against criminal ghost states, parastates, and CEAs will lie in foreign theaters—or in the skies over oceans and on the seas themselves. We already possess the material tools for the job. What we lack are innovative methodologies and adequately contemporary laws. To address the broad range of emerging threats, we don't need new weapons, just new rules of engagement. Our approach to future threats amounts to preparing for an outbreak of influenza when the world has cancer.

At present, we are ineffective combatants against emerging threats because of laws and practices that extend citizen-equivalent judicial treatment to foreign criminals who have had a far more savage effect on our country and its people than Saddam Hussein ever brought off. Eventually, we will recognize that international criminal and terrorist organizations in "peacetime" must be regarded as combatants during wartime: the goal is not to try them in a court of law, but to kill them until the survivors quit. Such a change in our practical approach to and interpretation of international law would be a far more potent weapon than any machine we could buy—and it is a more pressing requirement than we are collectively willing to acknowledge.

In summary, more and more governments are being overwhelmed by, run by, or supplanted by an astonishing variety of criminal organizations and innovative structures for controlling wealth through violence and coercion. Russian military and security ties to organized crime are already a noonday nightmare. Mexico's corruption is immeasurable; its government is ineffectual when not unwilling; its level of violence rises daily; and its effect on the United States can be measured in the number of alien inmates in our prisons, in the flow of drugs, in the brutalization of the cities, towns, and ranching communities of our Southwest, and in the decaying sovereignty of our southern land frontier. Brazil has lost control of much of its interior and of the impoverished cities within its cities. Europe's NATO states are flooded by criminal formations from former Warsaw Pact countries. Nigeria, an ambitious heroin broker, doesn't have an army—it has a mafia in uniform. Pakistan, that land of squandered legacies, is a violent, corrupt, feudal state held together only by the integrity of its army. The alarming trend among criminal organizations and other renegades is to cooperate—and they do it far better than the United Nations and NATO have managed in the wreckage of Yugoslavia.

Many of the countless conflicts around the world have no more than an emotional relevance to our national security, and we are foolish to give them more than a passing glance. We live in an age of such cataclysm and collapse, of such spiritual and material ruptures, that man's fate in the non-Western world will be settled only in blood, and contributing our blood would only make things worse, postponing resolution. But, as belabored above, some threats are already so immediate that we will have to confront them, like it or not.

And we will not like it.

The roles and missions of the U.S. military are going to change, but the changes will not have much to do with the legacy of the RMA. Flag officers, sensible colonels, and captains fresh from the sea can shake their heads, but the U.S. armed forces are already involved in struggles against international organized crime and illegal immigration. We deploy on missions of disease control, resource protection, security assistance, and the protection of U.S. citizens abroad. From fighting cholera in eastern Zaire to blocking our coastal waters against economic migrations, from fighting forest fires in the American West to evacuating our citizens from Liberia, impounding nuclear materials in Kazakhstan, and attempting to alter the patterns of Haitian or Balkan collective behavior, our military future is visible all around us. There are few conventional heroes. No wonder we yearn to refight the battle of Gettysburg.

Our armed forces long for "military" missions and struggle to keep the holy brotherhood pure. But, as they maneuver to avoid roles in "nonmilitary" problems, they betray the trust placed in them by the citizens they are pledged to protect. *A military's reason for being is to do its nation's dirty work.*

A watershed event was our military's adept refusal to play a direct role, rather than a safe supporting role, in counterdrug operations when the issue surfaced in the 1980s. Honorable, well intentioned, and desperate to protect the force from the high proportion of failures endemic to such efforts, a military leadership that remembered Vietnam too well successfully argued that counterdrug operations are a law-enforcement function. The Department of State, always wary of the military arm's reach, agreed. As a result, our direct-action counterdrug operations in the Andean Ridge come down to a few scattered handfuls of U.S. government agents charged with bringing down the most successful international business operation in Latin American history—while much of our hemisphere engages in a struggle to the death over the future shape of human societies.

Fighting drug cartels and combatting other criminal "ghost states" is the moral officer's nightmare, full of impossible restrictions, gray areas, and daily opportunities to embarrass the flag and demoralize the force. But is self-perpetuation the highest purpose of our military establishment? Drugs and drug-related violence have killed more Americans, wrecked more lives, and cost us more in real-dollar terms than did the Vietnam War. Our cities have been raped, and generations of the poor have been lost irretrievably. Doesn't that constitute a threat to our national security?

We are constrained by a past century's model of what armies do, what police do, and what governments legally can do. Our opponents have none of this baggage.

Of course, the military could not solve this problem alone. As remarked above, we are constrained by a past century's model of what armies do, what police do, and what governments legally can do. Our opponents have none of this baggage, whether they are druglords or warlords. CEAs and other nontraditional organizations increasingly can outspend, outmaneuver, outshoot, outnegotiate, and outthink states and their formal tools for enforcing order. For our part, we do not protect our most defenseless citizens from foreign enemies who penetrate our borders almost effortlessly. The relevant institutions of the U.S. government need to redefine themselves vis-à-vis the rest of the world, but we will probably fail to do it until the situation becomes so desperate that it threatens our elites and the money-buffered enclaves in which they live, learn, and work.

U.S. and international laws and appallingly outmoded diplomatic practices also cripple us in asymmetrical exchanges such as that which occurred in Somalia, just as they make a joke out of all efforts to bring a "just" end to the butchery in the former Yugoslavia. You cannot, cannot, cannot play by text-book rules when your opponent either hasn't read the book or has thrown it away. Attempts to bring our wonderful, comfortable, painstakingly humane laws and rules to bear on broken countries drunk with blood and anarchy constitute the ass end of imperialism.

In the nearer-than-currently-imaginable future, our happy-face attempts at peacekeeping are going to evolve into operations aimed at self-preservation. It is hard to bring this point home, since traditionalists can dismissively ask whether one foresees a radical Islamic fundamentalist invasion of Missouri or a Mexican raid on Wall Street (although one might argue that the peso collapse was just that), knowing that like-minded readers will nod approvingly and go back to keeping the world safe for defense contractors. But ours is a world in which fringe Islamists bomb the World Trade Center and crack cocaine haunts the streets of Kansas City. A large proportion of the Los Angeles rioters emboldened by the media's lionization of Rodney King were illegal immigrants. And the U.S. contingent in Mogadishu suffered proportionately more casualties than did the force that fought Desert Storm. This is a terribly changed and rapidly changing world.

The U.S. armed forces must change with that world and must change in ways that are fundamental—a new human understanding of our environment would be of far more use than any number of brilliant machines. We have fallen in love with the wrong revolution.

It is painful to write this. I personally love the Army as it is, valuing its ethos, its invigorating routine, its respect for our heritage. I love the legends and lineages, and a glimpse of our flag can move me profoundly. Selfishly, I do not want my Army to change, and my secret fantasies run more to Sherman at Shiloh than to tracking desperate, malnourished, and terrified economic refugees. I wish that the military that might descend safely from the RMA could be the sole answer to our nation's security challenges, but I cannot find grounds to believe it. It is a miserable prospect to be an officer faced with the need to argue in favor of filthy missions that will never entirely succeed and that will lend endless ammunition to those who loathe the institution that has given worth to my life. I wish it could be otherwise.

I understand the many reasons why it is preferable to think about, to write about, and to act upon the issues summed up by the phrase "Revolution in Military Affairs." To the earnest, the RMA offers an opportunity for engagement; to the careerist, it promises advancement and lucrative postmilitary employment; to the academic, it offers intellectual finiteness—concrete specifications rather than confounding ideas. The RMA—which I believe to be a historical event, whereas others consider it barely begun—allows the traditionalist to appear forward-minded and permits the forward-minded to avoid unpleasant realities. Most of the best minds within and surrounding the military have been drawn into RMA-related issues. Much of this effort is of great value, for we will, of course, always need to maintain conventional (or postconventional) forces. But perhaps just a few of those bright officers and analysts would better serve their country by taking an open-eyed look at the black, hideous, broken, career-destroying world around us.

The New Warrior Class

The soldiers of the U.S. Army are brilliantly prepared to defeat other soldiers. Unfortunately, the enemies we are likely to face through the rest of this decade and beyond will not be "soldiers," with the disciplined modernity that term conveys in Euro-America, but "warriors"—erratic primitives of shifting allegiance, habituated to violence, with no stake in civil order. Unlike soldiers, warriors do not play by our rules, do not respect treaties, and do not obey orders they do not like. Warriors have always been around, but with the rise of professional soldieries, their importance was eclipsed. Now, thanks to a unique confluence of breaking empire, overcultivated Western consciences, and a worldwide cultural crisis, the warrior is back, as brutal as ever and distinctly better armed.

The primary function of any civilization is to restrain human excess, and even Slavic socialism served a civilizing mission in this regard. But as the restraints of contemporary civilization recede and noncompetitive cultures fracture, victim-states often do not have the forces, and the self-emasculated West does not possess the will, to control the new warrior class arising in so many disparate parts of the world. We have entered an age in which entire nations are subject to dispossession, starvation, rape, and murder on a scale approaching genocide—not at the hands of a conquering foreign power but under the guns of their neighbors. Paramilitary warriors— thugs whose talent for violence blossoms in civil war—defy legitimate governments and increasingly end up leading governments they have overturned. This is a new age of warlords, from Somalia to Colombia, from Afghanistan to the Balkans. In Georgia an ex-convict became a kingmaker, and in Azerbaijan a warlord who marched on the capital with a handful of wheezing armored vehicles briefly became prime minister. In Chechnya, on the northern slopes of the Caucasus, a renegade general carved out the world's first state run entirely by gangsters—not the figurative gangsters of high Stalinism, but genuine black marketeers, murderers, drug dealers, and pimps—and then his tribal followers defeated the Russian army. Their warriors are the source of power for such chieftains, and the will of the populace, enervated and fickle, matters little when it matters at all.

The enemies we are likely to face . . . will not be "soldiers," . . . but "warriors"—erratic primitives of shifting allegiance, habituated to violence, with no stake in civil order.

This essay briefly considers who these new warriors are in terms of their social and psychological origins and examines the environment in which they operate. The objective is to provide an intellectual passport into the warrior's sullen world for U.S. military officers and defense analysts, who, given their cultural and professional conditioning, would much rather deal with more conventional threats. This is an alert message from a very dark place.

Most warriors emerge from five social pools that exist in some form in all significant cultures. These pools produce warriors who differ in their individual implacability and redeemability. This differentiation is key to understanding warriors— who outwardly may appear identical to one another—and helps identify human centers of gravity within warrior bands or movements.

First-pool warriors come, as they always have, from the underclass (although their leaders often have fallen from the upper registers of society). The archetype of the new warrior class is a male who has no stake in peace, a loser with little education, no legal earning power, no abiding attractiveness to women, and no future. With gun in hand and the spittle of nationalist ideology dripping from his mouth, today's warrior murders those who once slighted him, seizes the women who avoided him, and plunders that which he would never otherwise have possessed. Initially, the totemic effect of a uniform, however shabby and incomplete, and the half-understood rhetoric of a cause lend him a notion of personal dignity he never sensed before, but his dedication to the cause is rarely as enduring as his taste for spoils. He will, however, cling to his empowering military garb. For the new warrior class, many of whose members possess no skills marketable in peace, the end of fighting means the end of the good times.

The longer the fighting continues, the more irredeemable this warrior becomes. And as society's preparatory structures such as schools, formal worship systems, communities, and families are disrupted, young males who might otherwise have led productive lives are drawn into the warrior milieu. These form a second pool. For these boys and young men, deprived of education and orientation, the company of warriors provides a powerful behavioral framework. These are the foot soldiers of the expanding revolution or insurrection, the masses in the streets, yet their commitment, initially at least, is the weakest. Although some second-pool warriors can ultimately be gathered back into society, their savagery increases with the duration and intensity of the conflict. The average warrior who takes up a Kalashnikov at age thirteen is probably not going to settle down to finish out his secondary school education ten years later without a powerful incentive.

The third pool contains the opportunists, the entrepreneurs of conflict, whose great strength is their cynicism. When it is profitable or otherwise advantageous, they may speak beautifully of the greater cause—but their real cause is their personal gain in power, money, influence, and security. Although such men can often be "converted" by a display or application of power, they will be your allies only as long as you are strong, strict, evidently committed for the duration, and intrusive. In their own cultural context, these men generally possess the best and most varied intelligence networks of all the warrior groups, since they are not constrained by faction or even local morality. They will even operate beyond the blood ties of family, clan, or tribe that often limit the effectiveness and broader appeal of warrior groups. They are masters of timing and surprise. Often touched with a dark genius, these chameleons are immeasurably dangerous—and the most likely type of warrior to be underestimated as mere criminals or vulnerably corrupt. When the interest of Western actors fades, their lack of core values and sense of maneuver can leave these third-pool warriors— true warlords—in control of cities, regions, and entire countries after the men of conviction have served their purpose and been killed by us or through betrayals.

The fourth pool of warriordom consists of the patriots. These may be men who fight out of strong beliefs in ethnic, religious, or national superiority, or those who have suffered personal loss in the course of a conflict that motivates them to take up arms. Although these warriors are the easiest to reintegrate into civil structures—especially if their experience of violence is relatively brief—some of these men, too, will develop a taste for blood and war's profits (all of the warrior pools, or categories, are porous, and men can float between them or manifest multiple characteristics simultaneously). These "patriotic" warriors are the most individualized psychologically, and their redeemability depends on character, cultural context, and the depth of any personal loss, as well as on standard characteristics such as goal achievement in their conflict and perceived postwar opportunities for jobs and other societal rewards. Even when they are our enemies, they are heroes to their kind, and many a Western military policy has foundered on our inability to see the appeal of the upright man who hates us and who is willing to kill or be killed to drive us from his tormented land.

Dispossessed, cashiered, or otherwise failed military men form the fifth and most immediately dangerous pool of warriors. Officers, NCOs, or just charismatic privates who could not function in a traditional military environment, or who have emerged from a dissolving military establishment, these men bring other warriors the rudiments of the military art—just enough to inspire faith and encourage folly in many cases, although the fittest of these men become the warrior chieftains or warlords with whom we must finally cope on the battlefield, or in the jungles, streets, and sewers. These warriors are especially dangerous, not only because their skills heighten the level of bloodshed, but also because they provide a nucleus of internationally available mercenaries or gunmen for future conflicts. Given that most civil wars begin with the actions of a small fraction of the population (less than 1 percent might actively participate in or support the initial violence), any impassioned assembly of militants with cash will be able to recruit mercenary forces with ease and spark "tribal" strife that will make the brutality of Africa in the 1960s seem like some sort of Quaker peaceable kingdom.

Many a Western military policy has foundered on our inability to see the appeal of the upright man who hates us.

The mercenary trend is also on the rise in Western employ, and the advent of butchers' bands masked as corporations, from Eurasia to South Africa, demands constant scrutiny. A logo and a business card do not legitimize international murder.

Paradoxically, while the warrior seeks to hold society out of equilibrium for his own profit, he thus prevents society from offering him any alternative to the warrior life. In our century of massive postwar demobilizations, most receiving governments retained sufficient structure to absorb and assist their ex-soldiers. Helpfully, the soldiers of the great armies of the West rarely tasted war's spoils as does the warrior; rather, soldiers experienced war's sacrificial side. But the broken states in which warriors currently control the balance of power do not have the infrastructure to receive veterans and help them rebuild their lives. In many cases, the warrior's roots have been torn up, and since he is talented only at violence, his loyalty has focused on his warlord, his band of fellow warriors, or, simply, on himself. Even if the miracle of peace should descend permanently on the ruins of Yugoslavia, Liberia, Lebanon, Cambodia, or El Salvador, the survivor states will be unable to constructively absorb all the warriors who have fallen away from civilized norms—and the warriors themselves often have no real interest in being absorbed. In the Caucasus and Afghanistan, in Nicaragua, Haiti, and Sri Lanka, warriors without wars will create problems for a generation, if not longer.

In the centuries before the rise of modern professional armies, the European world often faced the problem of the warrior deprived of war. In the sixteenth century—another age of shattered belief systems—disbanded imperial armies spread syphilis and banditry across the continent, and the next century's Thirty Years War—waged largely by warriors and not by soldiers as we know them—saw the constant disbanding and re-formation of armies, with the *Soldateska* growing ever more vicious, unruly, and merciless. Arguably modern Europe's greatest trauma, the Thirty Years War formally ended in 1648, but its warriors continued to disrupt the continent until they found other wars in which to die, were hacked to death by vengeful peasants, or were hunted down like beasts by authorities who finally had caught their breath. Today's warriors have a tremendous advantage over their antique brethren in the struggle for survival, however: the West's pathetic, if endearing, concern for human life, even when that life belongs to a murderer of epic achievement.

For the U.S. soldier, vaccinated with moral and behavioral codes, the warrior is a formidable enemy. Euro-American soldiers in general learn a highly stylized, ritualized form of warfare, with both written and customary rules. We are at our best fighting organized soldieries that attempt a symmetrical response. But warriors respond asymmetrically, leaving us in the role of redcoats marching into an Indian-dominated wilderness. Despite the valiant and skilled performance of the U.S. Army Rangers, our most significant combat encounter in Mogadishu looked much like Braddock's defeat. Russian regulars were first "Little Big Horned" in Tajikistan by tribesmen who slipped across the Afghan border, then Moscow's draftees and professionals alike were massacred in the streets of Grozniy by archetypal warriors. The asymmetrics of conflict in Northern Ireland cancered the British military for three decades, and peace is yet a fragile hope. Around the world, conventional military establishments are discovering their limitations.

We are at our best fighting organized soldieries that attempt a symmetrical response. But warriors respond asymmetrically, leaving us in the role of redcoats marching into an Indian-dominated wilderness.

While the U.S. Army could rapidly devastate any band of warriors on a battlefield, few warlords would be foolish enough to accept such a challenge. Warriors usually stand and fight only when they know or believe that they have an overwhelming advantage. Instead, they snipe, ambush, mislead, and betray, attempting to fool the constrained soldiers confronting them into alienating the local population or allies, while otherwise simply hunkering down and trying to outlast the organized military forces pitted against them. U.S. soldiers are unprepared for the absolute mercilessness of which modern warriors are capable, and they are discouraged or prohibited by their civilian masters and their own customs from taking the kind of measures that might be effective against members of the warrior class.

The U.S. experience with warriors in Somalia was not a happy one, but the disastrous UN experience in Yugoslavia was worse. Imagining that they could negotiate with governments to control warrior excesses, the United Nations and other well-intentioned organizations pleaded with the men in suits in Belgrade, Zagreb, and Sarajevo to come to terms with one another. But the war in Bosnia and adjacent regions had degenerated to a point where many local commanders obeyed only orders that flattered them. It took a local military shift—a far more important factor than NATO aircraft—to bring an exhausted pause to the fighting. Now American soldiers patrol a landscape made safe for ethnic cleansing and belatedly hunt down warriors to bring them to court years after their excesses. Even if our efforts succeed beyond reasonable expectation, gunmen, gangs, and black marketeers will haunt the Balkan passes and urban alleys for years to come.

On the West Bank of the Jordan and in Gaza, the newly legitimized Palestinian authorities face formidable problems with two lost generations, unskilled or deskilled, whose heroes answer offers of dialogue with terror and for whom compromise appears equivalent to prostitution. Without the Intifada, many Palestinians, from teenagers to the chronologically mature, have no core rationale for their lives. At a virtually immeasurable cultural remove, Irish Republican Army terrorists remain heroes for men and women who prefer a lush myth of the past to the sober demands of the future. In Sri Lanka, many Tamil rebels will never be able to return to productive lives in a settled society—nor will many of the Khmer Rouge, Kashmiri separatists, Peruvian narco-Marxists, Mexican drug "cowboys," Angola's UNITA rebels, or any of Africa's other clan-based warriors masquerading behind the rank and trappings of true soldiers. Even in the United States, urban gang members exhibit warrior traits and may be equally impossible to reconcile to civilized order as it is generally valued in Euro-America. For the warrior, peace is the least desirable state of affairs, and he is inclined to fight on in the absence of a direct, credible threat to his life. As long as the warrior believes that he can survive on the outside of any new peace, he will view a continuation of warfare through criminal means as the most attractive alternative. And there is good reason for the warrior to decline to lay down his arms—the most persistent and ruthless warriors ultimately receive the best terms from struggling governments. Indeed, they sometimes manage to overthrow those governments and seize power when the governments tumble into crisis after failing to deliver fundamental welfare and security to the population.

Terrorists remain heroes for men and women who prefer a lush myth of the past to the sober demands of the future.

In addition to those warriors whose educations—however rudimentary—were interrupted, men who fall into the warrior class in adulthood often find their new situation far more pleasant than the manual labor for subsistence wages or chronic unemployment to which peace had condemned them. The warrior milieu allows pathetic misfits to lead lives of waking fantasy and remarkable liberties. Unlike organized militaries, paramilitary bands do not adhere to rigorous training schedules, and when they need privies, they simply roust out the locals at gunpoint and tell them where to dig. In the Yugoslav ruins, for instance, many of the patriotic volunteers (identical, whether Serb, Croat, or Bosnian Muslim) found that war gave them leisure, choice, and recognition, as well as a camaraderie they had never known in the past. The unemployed *Lumpenproletarier* from Mostar or Belgrade could suddenly identify with the action-video heroes he and his comrades admired between raids on villages where only women, children, and old men remained.

In Armenia, during a period of crisis for Nagorno-Karabakh, I encountered a local volunteer who had dyed his uniform black and proudly wore a large homemade swastika on his breast pocket, even though his people had suffered this century's first genocide. The Russian mercenaries who rent out their resentment over failed lives almost invariably seek to pattern themselves after Hollywood heroes, and even Somalia's warlords adorned themselves with Anglo nicknames such as "Jess" or "Morgan." This transfer of misunderstood totems between cultures has a vastly more powerful negative effect on our world than the accepted logic of human behavior allows. But then, we have entered an age of passion and illogic, an era of the rejection of "scientific" order. That is exactly what the pandemic of nationalism and fundamentalism is about. We are in an instinctive, intuitive phase of history, and such times demand common symbols that lend identity and reduce the need for more intellectualized forms of communication. Once, warriors wore runic marks or crosses on their tunics—today, they wear T-shirts with Madonna's image (it is almost too obvious to observe that one madonna seems to be as good as another for humanity). If there were two cultural artifacts in any given bunker in the Bosnian hills, they were likely to be a blond nude tear-out and a picture of Sylvester Stallone as Rambo. Many warriors, guilty of unspeakable crimes, develop such a histrionic self-image that they will drop just about any task to pose for a journalist's camera—the photograph is a totem of immortality in the warrior's belief system, which is why warriors sometimes take the apparently illogical step of allowing snapshots of their atrocities. In Renaissance Europe (and Europe may yet find itself in need of another renaissance), the typical *Landsknecht* wanted money, loot, women, and drink. His modern counterpart also wants to be a star.

Worldwide, the new warrior class already numbers in the millions. If the current trend toward state softening continues, the opening decades of the new millennium may see more of these warriors than soldiers in legitimate armies in the struggling regions of the world. Although exact figures will never be available, and statistics junkies can quibble endlessly as to how many warriors are really out there, the forest looks dark and ominous enough without counting each last tree. And perhaps the worst news comes right out of *Macbeth:* the trees are moving.

Warrior-mercenaries always moved. Irishmen fought for France and Hungary, Scots for Sweden and France, and Germans sold their unwashed swordarms to everyone from Palermo to Poland. Swiss mercenaries still guard the pope. But today's improved methods of travel allow warriors deprived of "their" war to fly or drive to the next promising misfortune.

Mujahedeen from Afghanistan, so recently adored by Americans, have turned up in Azerbaijan, and Russian brawlers with military educations have fought in Bosnia, Croatia, Georgia, Nagorno-Karabakh, Tajikistan, Africa, and Latin America and as enforcers for the internationalizing Russian mafia. One of the most intriguing characters I met in the Caucasus was an ethnic Armenian citizen of Lebanon who had been trained by the PLO in the Bekaa Valley to fight Turkic Azeris in Karabagh. The Azeri warriors he faced had been trained by entrepreneurial Russians and exasperated Turks, and reportedly by Iranians and Israelis. In Bosnia, mustered-out Warsaw Pact soldiers served in the same loosely organized units as adventure-seeking Germans and Frenchmen. Yugoslavia and the wars on Russia's crumpled frontiers have been vast training grounds for the warriors who will not be content without a conflict somewhere. While most warriors will attempt to maintain their privileges of violence on their own territory, within their own linguistic groups, the overall number of warriors is growing so quickly that even a small percentage migrating from trouble spot to trouble spot could present a destabilizing factor with which we have yet to reckon.

The U.S. Army will fight warriors far more often than it fights soldiers in the future. This does not mean that the Army should not train to fight other organized militaries—they remain the most lethal, although not the most frequent, threat. But it would be foolish not to recognize and study the nasty little men who will haunt the brutal little wars we will be called upon to fight within the career span of virtually every officer reading this text.

There are quite a few realistic steps we might take to gain a better grasp on these inevitable, if unwanted, opponents. First, we should begin to build an aggregate database that is not rigidly compartmented by country and region. We may deploy to the country where Warlord X has carved out his fief, or we may meet him or his warriors on the soil of a third-party state. The future may create allegiances and alliances that will confound us, but if we start now to identify likely players, that drab, laborious, critical labor may pay significant dividends one day. As a minimum, if we start files on warrior chieftains now, we will have richer background files on a number of eventual heads of state. Such a database will be a tough sell in a time of shrinking staffs and disappearing budgets, and analysts, accustomed to the luxury of intellectual routine, will rebel against its challenge and uncertainty. But in practical terms, studying potential opponents of this nature now will pay off on two counts: first, when we fight, we will be more likely to know whom we're fighting; second, the process of compiling such a database will build human expertise in this largely neglected field.

We also need to struggle against our American tendency to focus on hardware and bean counting to attack the more difficult and subtle problems posed by human behavior and regional history. For instance, to begin to identify the many fuses under the Caucasus powder keg, you have to understand that Christian Armenians, Muslim (and other) Kurds, and Arabs ally together because of their mutual legacy of hatred toward Turks. The Israelis support Turkic peoples because Arabs support the Christians (and because the Israelis are drawn to Caspian oil). The Iranians see the Armenians as allies against the Turks but are torn because Azeri Turks are Shi'a Muslims. And the Russians want everybody out who doesn't "belong." Many of these alignments surprise U.S. planners and leaders because we don't study the hard stuff. If electronic collection means can't acquire it, we pretend we don't need it—until we find ourselves in downtown Mogadishu with everybody shooting at us.

We need to commit more of our training time to warrior threats. But first we need to ask ourselves some difficult questions. Do we have the strength of will, as a military and as a nation, to defeat an enemy who has nothing to lose? When we face warriors, we will often face men who have acquired a taste for killing, who do not behave rationally according to our definition of rationality, who are capable of atrocities that challenge the descriptive powers of language, and who will sacrifice their own kind in order to survive. We will face opponents for whom treachery is routine, and they will not be impressed by tepid shows of force with restrictive rules of engagement. Are we able to engage in and sustain the level of sheer violence it can take to eradicate this kind of threat? Recent experience says no. Yet that answer may prove transient as administrations change and nontraditional threats multiply.

Although there are nearly infinite variations, the warrior threat generally requires a two-track approach—an active campaign to win over the populace, coupled with irresistible violence directed against the warlords and the warriors. You cannot bargain or compromise with warriors. You cannot "teach them a lesson" (unless you believe that Saddam Hussein or General Aideed learned anything worthwhile from our fecklessness in the clinch). You either win or you lose. This kind of warfare is a zero-sum game. And it takes guts to play.

Combatting warriors will force us to ask fundamental questions about ourselves as well as about our national and individual identities and values. But the kind of warfare we are witnessing now and will see increasingly in the future raises

. even more basic issues, challenging many of the assumptions in which Western culture indulges. The breakdown of Yugoslavia alone raised issues that have challenged philosophers and college freshmen since the first professor faced a lecture hall. What is man's nature? Are we really the children of Rousseau and of Benetton ads, waiting only for evil governments to collapse so that our peaceable, cotton-candy natures can reveal themselves? Or are we killing animals self-organized into the disciplinary structures of civilization because the alternative is mutual, anarchic annihilation? What of all that self-hobbling rhetoric about the moral equivalency of all cultures? Isn't it possible that a culture (or religion or form of government) that provides a functional combination of individual and collective security with personal liberties really does deserve to be taken more seriously than and emulated above a culture that glorifies corruption, persecutes nonbelievers, lets gunmen rule, and enslaves its women? Is all human life truly sacred, no matter what crimes the individual or his collective may commit?

Until we are able to answer such questions confidently, the members of the new warrior class will simply laugh at us and keep on killing.

Winning Against Warriors

One consequence of the diffusion of power at the end of the twentieth century has been the resurgence of the "warrior." In our lifetimes, this morally savage, unruly killer, not the trained, disciplined soldier, will be the type of enemy most frequently encountered by Euro-American militaries. Warriors have been present throughout history in various forms—tribesmen, mercenaries, terrorists, pirates, bandits, partisans, gangs—but their numbers increase and decrease in rhythm with historical cycles. In ages and places where relative equilibrium prevails, their numbers are fewer. But, to borrow a phrase from Thomas Hardy, "in the time of the breaking of nations," their numbers multiply.

Our century has been one of unprecedented cataclysm, which began as a struggle for empire and climaxed in a contest of systems of social organization. The victorious system held that man might successfully control the government above him, while the loser asserted that the destiny of government was to control the man below. The victory of democracy and market in much of the Northern Hemisphere simultaneously

48

exposed the inadequacy of any secular system to sate the hunger of man's religious impulse, made manifest in his yearning for destiny and belonging. In the brilliant states of the rich, a crisis of belief conditions the eye to see only democracy's flaws and the shortcomings of societies whose decency, if imperfect, is without parallel in human history. The Westerner adorns himself with imagined guilt.

In less fortunate regions, the Other Man rejects the codes of the West, even as he bitterly envies Western property and privilege. In prosperous and poverty-stricken lands alike, citizens who cannot climb into modernity, either from lack of skills or from fear of spiritual and structural dispossession, turn to fundamentalist forms of religion whose "certainties" are as unforgiving as they are occult, or to racial nationalism, or to both. In many places, the collapse of ordering structures permits the reemergence of brutal individual and collective forms of behavior that "civilized" men recently believed could be eradicated like smallpox. In this world of doubt and disorder, the warrior finds opportunity; in massacre, he finds inspiration; and from the fears of the weak and indecisive, he culls delicious power. He forces us to ask two great questions: What does civilization mean? What is civilization worth to us? On a bloody and immediate level, the warrior makes our soldiers ask how he can be defeated.

We see but do not understand—because nonrecognition of the human condition is our culture's great enabler. Cocooned by images and information that deconstruct horror into neutral symbols and language, we can enjoy data as entertainment without real emotional engagement. Anything that can be "known" without being felt is resistible. Even the fashionable Western sense of guilt mentioned above is about us, not them.

Professions of guilt for a mythologized responsibility vis-à-vis failed cultures are a luxury of the rich. If we are to be honest, the poor inmates of the un-Westernizable world have become exotic pets in the minds of those who have appointed themselves as our cultural consciences. Although the language has evolved, today's multiculturalists are the inheritors of the "little brown brothers" approach to human relations—since other cultures are not strong enough to defend themselves, we, the bright and white, will protect them along with the rain forests, elephants, and seal pups.

Public communicators facilitate this alienation. The languages of diplomacy and of the media are increasingly debased, and their unconscious function is no longer to communicate but to distance the receiver from experience, creating the psychological equivalent of a gated residential community. The patterns of our public language are consistently reductionist, seeking to impose commonalities on unique experience.

This is called civilization, and it is effective and generally good for us. Western mental constructs, for all of our multicultural drooling, allow us to touch selectively without being touched. It is a purpose of all successful civilizations to avoid understanding competitors, since the greatest ethical and practical freedom of action historically has been obtained by denying the Other a valid identity. Our current difficulty in dealing with warriors rises from our retention of this previously empowering ignorance of the Other while expecting it to coexist with our modern romanticizing of the non-West—we don't understand the warrior and we don't really want to hurt him. This is a poor starting point for a military intervention.

Decaying civilizations, such as that of Eurasian Islam, have it even worse—they cannot accept the reality of their own identity without collapsing. In any case, civilization is impossible without collective alienation from those beyond its physical or spiritual frontiers, and our robust culture answers this requirement by collecting vast amounts of data in order to avoid the need to understand on a direct human level. We choose not to understand the world on terms other than our own, although we occasionally lionize one set or another of not particularly deserving foreign victims for moral entertainment, as Lord Byron did the Greeks or the Western media have done with the Kurds, those geniuses of discord.

We Westerners respond to atrocity fitfully, we demote genocide to a photo opportunity (as long as it happens in a country whose residents are not white), and thugs have standing permission to commandeer noncompetitive states so long as they do not harm international business or stain our borders with immigrants. This is a system that usually works very well. But we do have a Judeo-Christian moral legacy that demands its psychological tax. So, when we are not too busy with the details of everyday life, we, the people, consider that it would be nice to put an end to some of that hurtsome behavior out there. It is a decent, if inchoate, impulse.

Our national leaders and other privileged Americans, whose children no longer wear their nation's uniform, feel an even more powerful urge to "do something" about Somalia or Rwanda or the Balkans or Haiti than does the average citizen (curiously, our elites are much more apt to feel sympathy for exotic foreigners than for their own less advantaged countrymen). But it is terribly difficult to identify exactly what is to be done, or how, to effect a worthwhile, enduring end.

There is intermittent alarm—without insight. We wish to act, but we are prisoners of our long habit of refusing to understand the forces upon which we mean to inflict our will. So we target a warlord and expect to change patterns of social interaction that have endured for centuries; we deploy the 10th Mountain Division, hoping to inspire good government; and we send peacekeepers—soldiers who hold less human reality for our own elites than do foreign refugees—to Balkan fiefdoms where no side will long tolerate a peace that allows its enemy to prosper.

In the American past, the use of military power meant that policy had failed. In America's present, the deployment of troops is a substitute for policy.

In the American past, the use of military power meant that policy had failed. In America's present, the deployment of troops is a substitute for policy. Our otherwise effective system of avoiding human knowledge of the inhabitants of other cultures stymies us when we have to deal with them on their turf and on their terms—while we remain imprisoned by laws and customs developed to deal with opponents within our own civilization. You can't fight the Somalis the same way you might fight the Swedes.

The behaviors in the non-Western world that so frustrate us are rooted in cultural values and religious beliefs—and perhaps even in biology, although our cult of the individual prevents us from examining that possibility. You cannot change any of this with bayonets—or even with sensitized peacekeepers reliant upon "nonlethal means." We do not think of ourselves as imperialists, of course, but what is it, really, when we dispatch troops

to country X for the purpose of imposing a system of government palatable to us without bothering to examine the belief
systems and received values of the target society?

Religion is the oldest form of government. It has provided
the foundation or at least the justification for subsequent
forms of government into the modern age (consider the stunning effectiveness of the Hindu religion as an ordering structure, with its divinely sanctioned caste system to guarantee
social discipline and resource allocation that favors the elite).
And what about cultural modalities that demand revenge or
prohibit compromise? What about those men, women, and
children who truly are not "like us," and whose beliefs, values,
taboos, prejudices, and practical behaviors are irreconcilably at
odds with our own? When will we recognize that a nuclear
device has a different resonance in the Indian mind than it
does in that of an American liberal? We do not think in terms
of a "Christian bomb," but real and potential opponents speak
unreservedly of their desire for an "Islamic bomb." Our greatest weakness is our refusal to acknowledge differences that
make us uncomfortable. In Washington, this leads to an occasional embarrassment. For our soldiers abroad, it leads to
humiliation and death. We fight for abstract values, practical
advantage, and a secular government. Increasingly, our enemies fight for God and revenge.

Our great sin is pride. We imagine that we should and can
make other peoples behave like us. And we intend to do this
without understanding who they are. Whether the people in
country X live in a surfeit of religious ecstasy or are waking
from the hard drunk of a secular "ism," military means applied
without insight will, at best, temporarily alter overt behavior.
But it will not change the essence.

A fundamental asymmetry exists because, despite our child-like enchantment with the notion of democracy for all people everywhere, we tend not to see those foreign masses whom we wish to bless as composed of individuals—even though we have, paradoxically, elevated the idealized Individual to the status of a mortal god within our own culture. Our least successful military interventions in this century attacked the cardinal identity of the native. What gives a man a sense of himself in his cultural context? When asked who he is, how does he reply? Is his elementary social self defined by clan membership, by religious subordination, by his position as head of family (and enforcer of female morality)? What "routine" Western actions are liable to threaten his sense of place in the world? Is that sense of place inextricably bound to behaviors that are completely antithetical to our goals?

We fight for abstract values, practical advantage, and a secular government. Increasingly, our enemies fight for God and revenge.

The first test applied in considering a foreign intervention should not be to measure the repugnance of the offender's behavior, but to ask why such behavior has come about. If it is the result of tribal, ethnic, or religious hatred, you will only be able to suppress it (if you are lucky), but not eliminate the cause. You will attain a decisive result only if you are willing to take sides and acquiesce in your ally's excesses. Otherwise, to achieve even moderate success—the relative absence of violence and the co-option of some variable percentage of the population—you likely will have to remain in the object country indefinitely as judge and jury, as velvet-gloved oppressor. When you leave, the old violence will begin again, often with increased savagery.

Haiti was a seductive example, and one that justifiably troubled American consciences, since the United States has so often interfered in the Haitian passion play. With black immigrants threatening to disrupt Florida's social and political balance, we finally sent troops. The Haitians watched with admiration, delighted with our nebulous promises of change. But what have we accomplished? What second act will make the population prosperous, literate, and tolerant enough for the Anglo-American brand of democracy we expect? Have political murders and oppression ceased forever? How many additional resources are we willing to expend? What roles have un-Western religious beliefs and cultural traits played in bringing Haiti to its transcendent squalor? What can we truly change? How much will be enough? What do we really want? Again, was our rhetorically selfless response to Haitian disorder about them in any meaningful respect, or only about us?

In Somalia, we faced warriors and found that their resilience in the face of massive casualties was greater than our political will as we suffered comparatively few. When decision makers realized, astonishingly belatedly, that this was a life-or-death struggle, they quit, wasting the lives of our soldiers and squandering the prestige of our state. And what had we expected our military presence to achieve? Whereas the initial mission was described as feeding the hungry, we actually believed that the mere display of our might would impress warlords into behaving corporately when they were in the midst of tribal feuds that had run so long there were no records of their beginnings. When our parade failed to change the nature of

Somalia, we began to shoot timidly. One is reminded of Joseph Conrad's image in *Heart of Darkness:* a puffing European gunboat shelling the opaque vastness of a continent.

From the military perspective, the scapegoat for Somalia was "mission creep." We deployed for one discrete purpose and found ourselves employed for a multiplicity of other missions. This is naive. U.S. ground forces will likely never again deploy abroad without experiencing the demands of mission creep. In Rwanda, the U.S. military leadership masterfully contained the pressures for an expansion of our mandate, but it was a near-run thing.

In Haiti, we went in to take out the political garbage and found ourselves picking up the literal garbage, an image that no doubt delighted Oliver Stone fans—those who crave any debasement of our military in order to justify their personal evasions.

In the purely military sphere, the dilemma of mission creep hearkens back to the maxim that no plan survives its first contact with reality. In its postmodern sense, mission creep arises from the universally unrealistic expectations of foreign peoples as to the U.S. military's capabilities; from the candy-store demands of allied armies, international baby-sitting collectives, and nongovernmental organizations; and from the lack of unifying structure in our own policies. Into this witch's brew, stir Clausewitzian *Friktion* gone mad. When that Prussian father of chaos and complexity studies articulated his theory of friction in war, he imagined only two contending militaries or military alliances operating according to symmetrical rules of behavior. In contemporary military interventions, there are often multiple warring parties, overlaid with civil factions, all interacting with multinational peacekeeping or peacemaking forces (often with radically different doctrines and agendas).

In capitals and at campsites, mutually competitive international organizations break from lecturing mass murderers to feud with nongovernmental relief agencies. Every one of these players responds, in turn, to the media. To imagine that the United States can send a company or a corps into such an environment with a clear, finite mission statement that will not evolve takes a remarkable mind.

Expeditionary planners must plan for mission creep. At a minimum, this demands plans that can flex, wholehearted commitment by the civilian leadership to see the mission through, and the realization by all that mission accomplishment may ultimately require many times the numbers of troops and lives originally envisioned.

Thus, a crucial step in winning against the warriors of the disturbed regions of the world is triage. First, we must seek to identify those cases in which the desired changes would require a revolution in indigenous values and beliefs. These are cases that cannot be resolved through military means, and however troubling it may be, the most humane and rational response is noninvolvement. Rwanda is an example of this class. Second, at the other end, are the overtly military conflicts that lend themselves to (at least provisional) resolution through military instruments. Desert Storm was a pertinent example. In the middle are the gray-area crises, in which there is a reasonable chance that military intervention will have a positive effect, and that the cost in friendly lives will not be disproportionate to the results. Panama was an example of this class of problem. Haiti may settle into a relatively benign period of social and economic stasis—an acceptable result, if we are to be honest—but the long-term odds are very much against any success in changing Haitian culture.

The assessment of gray-area problems also raises the issue of whether military interventions are not most effective either within their own cultural context or in closely related cultures, but increasingly less effective as the target country moves away from the interventionist's cultural base. There is already tacit recognition of this in our political support for or quiet approbation of regional coalitions taking on regional problems, as in Africa. This model cannot, however, rely only on superficial manifestations of cultural difference; it must look deeper toward motivational and value similarities. The military should be looking for a few good anthropologists.

For instance, the United States' post–World War II redesign of Japanese government and the corresponding reorientation of Japanese macrosociety were effective because of underlying similarities in values that were not so apparent in overt behavior, because of the target country's desire to evolve into greater "Westernness," and thanks to General Douglas MacArthur's incisive grasp of what could and should be altered and what needed to be left alone. Of MacArthur, a man of immense complexity, it might be said, "He came, he saw, he understood."

Despite the instant revisionism of the media, the same could be repeated of General Norman Schwarzkopf, who triumphantly managed a wartime alliance that included some members that were incandescently despicable. In the cases of both these leaders, the character flaws so appetizing to the deconstructionist press may have been inextricably linked to their abilities to deal with hierarchical cultures. Imagine either mission replayed with an equal-opportunity magnate in command. In any case, gray-area interventions and multicultural alliance operations alike demand both exceptional leadership and the empathy to intellectually and emotionally enter the other's culture.

Ultimately, the deciding factor for intervention in gray-area conflicts should be whether there is a genuine threat to the interests of the United States. If there is not, there is no justification for the attendant sacrifice of U.S. lives. Soldiers are citizens, too. Our current practice of whimsical intervention is morally indefensible—akin to shopping for body parts—and worse, after having served us so well for so long, it has become practically ineffectual. Yet the reality is that we will go, whether or not we can effect enduring good, and military leaders will have to make the best of bad missions and strive to bring home as many of their subordinates as possible.

How do we combat the warrior in these gray-area conflicts, where he is alive and all too well?

The anti-soldier comes from unstable combinations of five source pools, whether the conflict occurs at the tribal level or in the ruins of a once "modern" state. The first-pool warriors come from the underclass of society and are men (or women) with no stake in peace. Usually, they have little education and no marketable skills. Often, they are misfits in social relationships. Warrior status grants them recognition—a transformed sense of identity—and comradeship, as well as more tangible rewards. For these losers co-opted into the striking arm of a cause, whether they become Hitler's Brownshirts, Balkan rapists, or African mass murderers, the end of conflict means the end of the good times.

Second-pool warriors are "course-of-conflict" joiners, members of disrupted societies whose education or employment has been interrupted. Normally, they would have continued as productive citizens, but in the course of the Intifada or during the breakdown of traditional structures of order in Liberia, opportunities disappeared and peer pressure to join the struggle increased. For these warriors, membership in the warrior group is often simply a means of self-preservation, since, in many cultures, the mentality prevails that "he who is not with us is against us."

Opportunists, the "entrepreneurs of conflict," form the third source pool. Numerically, this is the smallest group, but its members are often the most incisively intelligent and operationally effective, since they are ultimately unencumbered by commitment to a greater cause. These opportunists often have criminal ties—if they are not outright criminals themselves. Whether we consider *narcotraficantes* or Josef Stalin, these opportunists display a genius for sensing power vacuums and exploiting them.

The fourth pool is the home of the true believers. These can be independence-seeking rebels or bitter racists, religious zealots, or charismatic figures diseased with the worst symptoms of ethnic nationalism. When we share a coincidence of beliefs and goals, these can be the easiest warriors with whom to deal; however, in the non-Western world, there is more often a chasm between our values and identities and theirs, making these men, to us, implacable and savage. They often fill leadership roles—at least until an entrepreneur or military figure takes over—and they invest their lives, and deaths, in the struggle for their cause. These are the men who defend the last mountain cave to their final breath, and were it not for their penchant for atrocity and the hatreds burning at the core of their being, we would have to admire their courage and fortitude. These are the assassination plotters of Algeria's radical Islamic underground and of Sendero Luminoso, the suicide bombers and the instigators of tribal massacre—but they are also the men who can inspire a people to arrest a country's dis-solution.

The last pool from which today's warriors arise is the military. As governments decay or as armies are drastically reduced in size, men trained in the use of arms are left to their own devices, and some of them regress to more primitive states. Often, the skills of violence are the only skills they know. These men find that they cannot fit in with civilian society, or choose to reject the diminution of stature that often comes with demobilization. Many of these men fit the traditional mercenary model, while others succumb to the promise of glory and vengeance dispensed by the true believers. A few may become successful entrepreneurs of conflict. They may end as dicta-tors—or as backcountry brigands.

Whatever their ultimate paths, these warriors with military skills increase the efficiency of violence. They may not know how to repair state-of-the-art aircraft, but they know how to lay a machine gun or range a mortar. Increasingly, fifth-pool war-riors also come with arms-trade connections. The breakup of the Soviet Union and the starvation and dismemberment of its military machine threaten to flood at least the regional market with such men. With the successive waves of decolonization in this century, many of the warriors from the military pool—men who learned the outward forms of soldiering in colonial ranks but never got the inner ethos—maneuvered themselves into power in newly independent states. This phenomenon was especially virulent in Africa.

Although they are not a separate category for analytical purposes, the increase in child warriors worldwide is an espe-cially troubling phenomenon. Whether Charles Taylor's Small Boy's Unit in Liberia, Iranian children squandered in wave attacks against the Iraqi military of the last decade, or the slightly older teenage *sicario* assassins of Colombia, the use of the young for the conduct of violence has an especially evil smell about it. These child warriors have unformed value systems and no sense of their own mortality. They torment and kill without remorse, indescribably ruthless in their naiveté (or instinctive state?), and are especially hard to redeem for society after a conflict closes.

More and more often, cynical or cause-intoxicated warlords appear to realize the shock value and utility of babes in arms, and increasingly, U.S. military personnel will have to confront them. This poses two serious problems. First, we are not conditioned to kill children. Yet if attacked with deadly force, we will have to do it, and it will sicken us—sometimes to the point of disaffection for the mission or even our calling. Second, whenever a U.S. military member pulls the trigger on a child wielding an automatic rifle or hand grenade, there is apt to be a journalist with a camera of some description in the area. No matter how justified the soldier's act of self-defense may have been, it will not look very attractive on network news, magazine covers, and newspaper front pages. For a significant segment of the U.S. and world populations, such images will destroy the credibility of our mission.

These warriors are our new, old enemy. If we think our actions through, avoid utterly hopeless gestures, plan well, and act decisively, we can beat them. Understanding the differences in motivations between warriors from the different pools described above is useful in defeating them, and there is one tried-and-true technique that can work against most of them. But before describing that method and its requirements, the stage must be set by highlighting the sort of operations that absolutely do not work: "politically correct operations," or PC-OPS, of the amorphous, foolish sort we attempted in Somalia, or through which everybody with a fax machine and frequent-flyer miles attempted to play savior of Bosnia. Making nice with hick bullies is unworthy of a superpower—or any rule-of-law state. Yet we insist on laborious, carefully articulated negotiations with mass murderers and criminals whose boots leave bloodstains on the carpet. We insist on playing by the rules of Metternich, while our enemies rule with the meat-ax. We are prisoners of a diplomatic mentality that conjures counterparts where no worthy opposite numbers exist. As a result, men like Milosevic, Aideed, Saddam, and countless narco-criminals frustrate our hopes and outlast our efforts.

The problem is that America wants to talk to its enemies. With the ascendancy of the Department of State in our neo-Wilsonian era, a legalistic view of the world prevails in which present borders are sacrosanct, any state is better than no state, any election is better than no election, and it is assumed that all men are ultimately reasonable and can be tamed through negotiations. In fact, much of the world is increasingly lawless, borders are breaking down from West Africa to Central Asia, elections have become the means to justify repression in much of the non-Western world, and warlords and demagogues are not only intractably unreasonable but also insatiable. We truly believe that all men want peace. This is nonsense. From the Andean Ridge to the High Caucasus, gunmen flourish under conditions of conflict. Even when they do want peace, it is not the peace of our imagination, but the peace of the fist.

Nor do warriors and warlords much care for the niceties of legal documents. They will agree to whatever is expedient when pressed, sign on the dotted line, then disavow the treaty, accord, or agreement the moment they intuit an advantage in doing so. Also, green-table agreements often have no meaning, because political figureheads or even warlords do not fully control their subordinates. President Y signs a cease-fire in Geneva, but the irregulars in the hills and contested cities of country Z pay it no mind. In the ruins of Yugoslavia, each side learned to manipulate Western diplomats, officials, and do-gooders, exploiting our humanitarian biases, vanities, and ineradicable gullibility. The Bosnian Serbs repeatedly played ambassadors off against special envoys against the media, with the result that military forces deployed to the region were frozen in place by talk, promises, and diplomatic self-delusion. Today, Bosnia is a stalemate pretending to be a solution, and Serbs in Kosovo are repeating the behavior that won them international condemnation but achieved their goals. Our diplomatic successes have come when we adjusted our own goals to the local demands—we have not stopped any fighting until the fighters were ready to stop.

We send our military into a broken country to "lend credibility" to our diplomatic efforts. But the moment the local warriors realize that our military will not be employed as such or will not be used to full effectiveness, the credibility is gone.

The diplomats we allow to budget our soldiers' lives are not much of a match for warriors, the first enchained by civilization and the latter possessed of the vitality and freedom that the strong and unscrupulous discover in civilization's overthrow.

In desperation, we send our military into a broken country to "lend credibility" to our diplomatic efforts. But the moment the local warriors realize that our military will not be employed as such or will not be used to full effectiveness, the credibility is gone—and the threat of sending in the Marines has already been squandered as a tool of persuasion. We must get back to the realization that, as then Major General Leonard Wood said perfectly in 1912, "the purpose of an army is to fight." If we do not mean to fight, we should not send in the military, except for disaster relief where the host country is receptive and other brief, focused, and exceptional humanitarian efforts. When we do choose a military option, the military must have the lead, both in combat and in any further negotiations. Without unity of command and unity of effort, we cannot beat the warrior.

A technique that can work against warriors is the "strategy of separation." This has ancient roots and is further shaped by recent counterinsurgency experience. Understanding the varied societal origins and motivations of warriors lets us refine it. Simply put, this is the technique that General George Crook used against the Indians and that the U.S. Army employed against the Moros—cut them off from their sources of strength and pursue them relentlessly. In modern practice, operations may be more complex, but the fundamentals have not changed.

The fundamental requirement is a thorough understanding of the culture—the social psychology, normative behaviors, rituals, and core beliefs—of the target country or region. Who supports the warrior, and why? What actions will lessen that support, and what blunders of ours might increase it? Who are the society's heroes, and why? How do we avoid turning a murderous warlord into a rallying point or martyr? The questions could go on until they doubled the length of this essay, but the point is simply that, if you intervene ignorant of the underlying local conditions, you will likely fail—and you will certainly pay in blood.

The first concrete step is to separate the warriors from the population. The techniques for doing this will vary from society to society, from mission to mission, but the warrior cannot be allowed to "swim in the sea of the people," nor can he be allowed to draw on popular resources for his struggle. The warrior must be separated from the population both physically and psychologically. The next step is to peel away those warriors who are not fully committed to the cause. The course-of-conflict joiners can be drawn off by a combination of enticements and demonstrated threats, while opportunists will desert the cause when they realize that continued opposition will cost them not only their material gains but their lives. Faced with combat in which they suffer obviously disproportionate casualties, many of the warriors from the underclass will leave the fight (although their warrior behavior may persist in a criminal subculture, which can be dealt with later).

In some situations, when we are particularly incisive and have good intelligence, we may even be able to create rifts between those warriors with military backgrounds and the true believers, for instance, by creating circumstances in which the true believers feel obliged to fight for a symbolic objective, while the military-trained warriors recognize it as suicidal. But at this point, both great skill and luck are required, and we will frequently have to be content with successes below this level.

The final step is to neutralize the remainder. This is a military problem and requires a military solution. Although much of our military technology is of little utility in the initial phases of such an intervention, it becomes increasingly useful in proportion to our success. When we have reduced the active warrior population to its fanatical inner circle, we have also reached a point where relentless military operations can bring victory. In pursuing the warriors, by driving them until they are continually harried and exhausted, increasingly short of war-making materiel, and even physically hungry, we can break them and beat them. This pursuit phase, which may last weeks or months, is when we can more fully exploit technology—our surveillance systems, helicopters, smart weapons—and our superior resources in materiel, firepower, and numbers to stage continuous operations (we accept that a fight like Desert Storm demands around-the-clock operations, but these must also become the norm in fighting warriors). Above all, the warrior cannot be given any respite.

This is really where the problem picks up again. Because of the belief prevalent among Western elites that negotiations can ultimately solve any problem, because the warrior can play to our well-meant humanitarianism, and because the diplomats will want to be in on the kill, the most difficult challenge of the entire operation will be to prevent politically imposed cease-fires before the warrior is thoroughly defeated. The worse his situation becomes, the more apt he will be to agree to talk, to compromise, to stop shooting as long as he can retain his arms. It will be tempting. But the rule must be no negotiations until surrender. We may publish and broadcast magnanimous surrender terms throughout our intervention, but we cannot allow the warrior to catch his breath. Either he surrenders—and is treated with the legal decency guaranteed by U.S. practice and international conventions—or he faces the full might of the American military machine. Cease-fires just short of victory historically have squandered all previous efforts.

The key to making this strategy work is the education of our domestic decision makers. Before a single soldier deploys, we must clearly and responsibly articulate the problem facing us and the steps required to bring about a solution. We in the military must offer an intelligible plan and convince our superiors and co-actors to sign up for it. All the players must agree in advance that this will be our strategy and that we will stick to it unless it manifestly fails. It is not a strategy for the fickle, but any strategy will founder on indecisiveness. An attractive aspect of an approach such as separation of the warrior from his base followed by relentless pursuit is that it can be espoused as doctrine, so that friends and enemies alike know what to expect. Although we will not want to tip the hour of our advance party's arrival in every case, we can, at the right moment, explain the broad contours of our plan to the press and the public. In fact, publicity for our approach—especially for generous surrender terms and amnesties for those who have not committed atrocities—helps the effort considerably. While the details of military movements and tactical actions will remain classified until they are completed, our efforts can otherwise profit from transparency: mess with the United States, and this is what you get.

All interventions will have individual characteristics and eccentric requirements. All plans will change, and political reality will have its day. But we must begin to take a more ordered approach to the warrior problem, if only to avoid making heroes of scoundrels, as we did with "General" Aideed, or squandering the lives of our military as a substitute for policy, as we did in Beirut. In an age when the most materially fortunate families in our society would not dream of sending their sons and daughters to serve in the military, those children of privilege, when they inevitably occupy positions of power in our government, will be understandably naive when it comes to the capabilities and limitations of the military arm. Whereas once it was a tacit function of military establishments to educate the lower classes and immigrants in "Americanness," it now has become our duty to educate the best and the brightest on how to deal with the worst and the darkest.

Timing is the key. Just as traditional military wisdom holds that it is nearly impossible to recover from flawed initial dispositions, so it is often disastrous to try to improvise policy and plans after the military has already been deployed to some ruptured foreign land. Our country deserves sound doctrine from the military. We in the military deserve firm decisions from our superiors. It is a pressing task of the U.S. military to offer designs for decision that win the trust of the people and the president alike—and to speak honestly when we believe that the military is not part of the solution.

Our Soldiers, Their Cities

The future of warfare lies in the streets, sewers, high-rise buildings, industrial parks, and sprawl of houses, shacks, and shel-
ters that form the broken cities of our world. We will fight
elsewhere, but not so often, rarely as reluctantly, and never so
brutally. Our recent military history is punctuated with city
names—Tuzla, Mogadishu, Los Angeles, Beirut, Panama City,
Hue, Saigon, Santo Domingo—but these encounters have
been but a prologue, with the drama still to come.

We declare that only fools fight in cities and shut our eyes
against the future. But in the next century, in an uncontrol-
lably urbanizing world, we will not be able to avoid urban
deployments short of war and even full-scale city combat.
Cities have always been centers of gravity, but they are now
more magnetic than ever before. Once the gatherers of
wealth, then the processors of wealth, cities and their satellite
communities have become the ultimate creators of wealth.
They concentrate people and power, communications and
control, knowledge and capability, rendering all else periph-

eral. They are also the postmodern equivalent of jungles and mountains—citadels of the dispossessed and irreconcilable. A military unprepared for urban operations across a broad spectrum is unprepared for tomorrow.

The U.S. military, otherwise magnificently capable, is an extremely inefficient tool for combat in urban environments.

The U.S. military, otherwise magnificently capable, is an extremely inefficient tool for combat in urban environments. We are not doctrinally, organizationally, or psychologically prepared, nor are we properly trained or equipped, for a serious urban battle, and we must task organize radically even to conduct peacekeeping operations in cities. Romantic and spiritually reactionary, we long for gallant struggles in green fields, while the likeliest "battlefields" are cityscapes where human waste goes undisposed, the air is appalling, and mankind is rotting.

Poor state or rich, disintegrating society or robust culture, a global commonality is that more of the population, in absolute numbers and in percentage, lives in cities. Control of cities has always been vital to military success, practically and symbolically, but in our postmodern environment, in which the wealth of poor regions as well as the defining capabilities of rich states are concentrated in capitals and clusters of production-center cities, the relevance of nonurban terrain is diminishing in strategic, operational, and even tactical importance—except where the countryside harbors critical natural resources. But even when warfare is about resource control, as in America's Gulf War, simply controlling the oil fields satisfies neither side.

The relevant urban centers draw armies for a slew of reasons, from providing legitimacy and infrastructural capabilities, to a magnetic attraction that is more instinctive than rational (perhaps even genetically absorbed at this point in the history of mankind), on to the fundamental need to control indigenous populations—which cannot be done without mastering their urban centers. We are entering a new age of assaults on cities, but one in which the siege techniques would be largely unrecognizable to Mehmet the Conqueror or Vauban, and the parameters incomprehensible to our own greatest conquerors of cities, Ulysses S. Grant and Winfield Scott.

Consider just a few of the potential trouble spots where U.S. military intervention or assistance could prove necessary in the next century: Mexico; Colombia; the subcontinent with an expansionist, nuclear India; the Arabian Peninsula; Brazil; or the urbanizing Pacific Rim. Even though each of these states or regions contains tremendous rural, desert, or jungle expanses, the key to each is control of an archipelago of cities. The largest of these metropolitan areas have populations in excess of twenty million today—more specific figures are generally unavailable as beleaguered governments lose control of their own backyards. Confronted with an armed and hostile population in such an environment, the U.S. Army as presently structured would find it difficult to muster the dismount strength necessary to control a single center as simultaneously dense and sprawling as Mexico City.

Step down from the level of strategic rhetoric about the future, where anyone with self-confidence can make a convincing case for his or her agenda. Survey instead the blunt, practical ways in which urban combat in today's major cities would differ from a sanitary anomaly such as Desert Storm or the never-to-be-fought third European civil war in the German countryside, where we pretended urban combat could be avoided, and for which so much of the equipment presently in our inventory was designed.

At the broadest level, there is a profound spatial difference. "Conventional" warfare has been horizontal, with an increasing vertical dimension. In fully urbanized terrain, however, warfare becomes profoundly vertical, reaching up into towers of steel and cement and downward into sewers, subway lines, road tunnels, communications tunnels, and the like. Even with the "emptying" of the modern battlefield, organizational behavior in the field strives for lateral contiguity and organizational integrity. But the broken spatial qualities of urban terrain fragments units and compartmentalizes encounters, engagements, and even battles. The leader's span of control can easily collapse, and it is very, very hard to gain and maintain an accurate picture of the multidimensional "battlefield."

Noncombatants, without the least hostile intent, can overwhelm the force, and there are multiple players beyond the purely military, from criminal gangs to the media, vigilante and paramilitary factions within militaries, and factions within those factions. The enemy knows the terrain better than the visiting army, and it can be debilitatingly difficult to tell friend from foe from the disinterested. Local combat situations can change with bewildering speed. Atrocity is close-up and commonplace, whether intentional or incidental. The stresses on the soldier are incalculable. The urban combat environment is, above all, disintegrative.

The modern and postmodern trend in Western militaries has been to increase the proportion of tasks executed by machines while reducing the number of soldiers in our establishments. We seek to build machines that enable us to win while protecting or distancing the human operator from the effects of combat. At present, however, urban combat remains extremely manpower intensive—and it is a casualty producer. Although a redirection of research and development efforts toward addressing the requirements of urban combat could eventually raise our efficiency and reduce casualties, machines probably will not dominate urban combat in our lifetimes, and the soldier will remain the supreme weapon. In any case, urban warfare will not require substantial numbers of glamorous big-ticket systems but great multiples of small durables and disposables whose production would offer less fungible profit margins and whose relatively simple construction would open acquisition to genuinely competitive bidding.

Casualties can soar in urban environments. Beyond those inflicted by enemy action, urban operations result in broken bones, concussions, traumatic-impact deaths, and, with the appalling sanitation in many urban environments, a broad range of septic threats. Given the untempered immune systems of many of our soldiers, even patrol operations in sewer systems that did not encounter an enemy could produce debilitating, even fatal, illnesses. One of many potential items of soldier equipment for urban warfare might be antiseptic biosheathing that coats the soldier's body and closes over cuts and abrasions, as well as wounds. Any means of boosting the soldier's immune system could prove to be a critical "weapon of war."

Urban warfare differs even in how "minor" items such as medical kits and litters should be structured. Soldiers need new forms of "armor"; equipment as simple as layered-compound knee and elbow pads could dramatically reduce the sort of injuries that, while not life-threatening, can remove soldiers from combat for hours, days, weeks, or even months. Eye protection is essential, given the splintering effects of firefights in masonry and wood environments, and protective headgear should focus as much on accidental blows from falls or collapsing structures as on enemy fire, on preserving the body's structural integrity as much as on protecting against ballistic threats.

Communications requirements differ, too. Soldiers need more comms distributed to lower levels—down to the individual soldier in some cases. Further, because of loss rates in the give-and-take of urban combat, low-level comms gear should not be part of the encrypted command and control network. Radios or other means of communication do not need extended range, but they must deal with terrible reception anomalies. Even a "digitized" soldier, whose every movement can be monitored, will require different display structures in the observing command center. This is the ultimate three-dimensional chessboard at the tactical level.

On the subject of command and control, the individual soldier must be even better trained than at present. He will face human and material distractions everywhere—it will be hard to maintain concentration on the core mission. Soldiers will die simply because they were looking the wrong way, and even disciplined and morally sound soldiers disinclined to rape can lose focus in the presence of female or other civilians whom they feel obliged to protect or who merely add to the human "noise level." The leader-to-led ratio must increase in favor of rigorously prepared low-level leaders. Whereas higher-level command structures may flatten, tactical units must become webs of pyramidal cells capable of extended autonomous behavior in a combat environment where multiple engagements can occur simultaneously and in relative isolation in the same building.

Nonsensical arguments about the Wehrmacht making do without so many NCOs and officers on the battlefield must be buried forever; not only is the German military of the last European civil war ancient history, but it lost decisively. Our challenge is to shape the U.S. Army of the twenty-first century.

Personal weapons must be compact and robust, with a high rate of fire and very lightweight ammunition, but there is also a place for shotgun-like weapons at the squad level. Overall, soldier loads must be reduced dramatically at the edge of combat, since fighting in tall buildings requires agility that a soldier unbalanced by a heavy pack cannot attain; further, vertical fighting is utterly exhausting and requires specialized mobility tools. Soldiers will need more upper body strength and will generally need to be more fit—this includes support soldiers, as well.

Ideally, each infantry soldier would have a thermal or post-thermal imaging capability—since systems that require ambient light are not much good thirty meters below the surface of the earth. Also, an enhanced ability to detect and define sounds could benefit the soldier—although he would have to be well trained to be able to transcend the distracting quality of such systems. Eventually, individual soldiers may have tactical equipment that can differentiate between male and female body heat distributions and will even be able to register hostility and intent from smells and sweat. But such devices will not be available for the next several interventions, and we will have to make do for a long time to come with soldiers who are smart, tough, and disciplined.

The roles of traditional arms will shift. Field artillery, so valuable elsewhere, will be of reduced utility—unless the U.S. military were to degenerate to the level of atrocity in which the

Russians indulged themselves in Grozniy. Until artillery further enhances accuracy, innovates warheads, and overcomes the laws of ballistic trajectories, it will not have a significant role in urban combat divisions. Because of attack angles and the capabilities of precision munitions, airpower will prove much more valuable and will function as flying artillery. Mortars, however, may be of great use, given their steep trajectories. More accurate and versatile next-generation mortars could be a very powerful urban warfare tool.

The bulk of tactical firepower will need to come from large-caliber, protected, direct-fire weapons. This means tanks, or future systems descended from the tank. Although today's tanks are death traps in urban combat—as the Russians were recently reminded—the need for protected, pinpoint firepower is critical. Instead of concentrating entirely on obsolescent rural warfare, armor officers should be asking themselves how the tank should evolve to fight in tomorrow's premier military environment, the city. First, the "tank" will need more protection, and that protection will need to be distributed differently—perhaps evolving to tuned electronic armor that flows over the vehicle to the threatened spot. Main guns will need to be large caliber, but ideally will be able to fire reduced-caliber ammunition as well, through a "caliber tailoring" system. Crew visibility will need to be greater. The tank will not need to sustain high speeds but will need a sprint capability. Further, the tank will need to be better integrated into local intelligence awareness.

Although the need for plentiful dismounted infantry will endure, those soldiers will intermittently need means for rapid, protected movement. But this does not necessarily mean mechanized infantry; rather, it may demand armored transport centralized at the division level on which the infantry trains, but that does not rob the infantry of man-power in peacetime or in combat.

Engineers will be absolutely critical to urban combat, but they, too, will need evolved tools and skills. The vertical dimension is only part of the challenge. Engineers will need to develop expanded skills, from enabling movement in developed downtown areas to firefighting. Demolition skills will be essential but will be a long way from blowing road craters. Tomorrow's combat engineers may have to drop twenty-story buildings on minimal notice under fire while minimizing collateral damage.

Aviation is vital to mobility, intelligence, and the delivery of focused firepower in urban environments, but as Mogadishu warned us, present systems and tactics leave us highly vulnerable. Rotary-wing aviation for urban combat does not need great range or speed but demands a richer defensive suite, great agility, and increased stealthiness.

Military intelligence must be profoundly reordered to cope with the demands of urban combat. From mapping to target acquisition, from collection to analysis, and from battle damage assessment to the prediction of the enemy's future intent, intelligence requirements are far tougher to meet in urban environments than on traditional battlefields. The utility of the systems that paid off so richly in Desert Storm collapses in urban warfare, and the importance of human intelligence (HUMINT) and regional expertise soars. From language skills to a knowledge of urban planning (or the lack thereof), many of the abilities essential to combat in cities are given low, if any, priority in today's intelligence architecture. Although leaders are aware of these shortfalls, military intelligence is perhaps more a prisoner of inherited Cold War structures than is any

other branch—although field artillery and armor are competitive in their unpreparedness for the future.

Military intelligence is at a crossroads today and must
decide whether to continue doing the often irrelevant things
it does so well or to embrace a realistic future that will
demand a better balance between systems and soldiers in a
branch particularly susceptible to the lure of dazzling
machines. Try templating an irregular enemy unit in urban
combat in the center of Lagos after twenty-four hours of contact. This does not mean that high-tech gear and analytical
methodologies are useless in urban environments. On the
contrary, innovative technologies and organizational principles could make a profound difference in how military intelligence supports urban combat operations. But we would need
to shift focus and explore radical departures from the systems
we currently embrace.

Military police and civil affairs troops will continue to play
the important roles they played in urban interventions during
the twentieth century, but psychological operations (PSYOPS)
units, long a stepchild, will surge in importance and may ultimately merge fully with military intelligence to enhance syn-
ergy and efficiency. Especially given the potential for electronic
population control systems in the next century, PSYOPS may
function as a combat arm, even if not credited as such.

Even supply is different. While deliveries do not need to
be made over great distances, soft vehicles are extremely vulnerable in an environment where it is hard to define a front
line and where the enemy can repeatedly emerge in the rear.
All soldiers will be fighters, and force and resource protection
will be physically and psychologically draining. Urban environments can upset traditional balances between classes of

supply. There may be less of a requirement for bulk fuel, but an intervention force may find itself required to feed an urban population or to supply epidemic-control efforts. Artillery and antitank guided missile expenditures might be minimal, while main gun and infantry systems ammunition consumption could be heated. Urban combat breaks individual and crew-served weapons and gear, from rifles to radios, and masonry buildings are even harder on uniforms than on human bones. Soldiers will need replacement uniforms far more often than during more traditional operations. Unfortunately, we also will need more replacement soldiers, and all combat support and combat service support troops are more apt to find themselves shooting back during an urban battle than in any other combat environment.

Where do we begin to prepare for this immediate and growing challenge? There are two powerful steps we ought to take. First, the U.S. Army should designate two active divisions and at least one National Guard division as urban combat divisions and should begin variable restructurings to get the right component mix. Rule one should be that the active divisions are not "experimental" in the sense of nondeployable, but remain subject to short-notice deployment to threatened urban environments. This would put an incredible stress on the unit and, especially, on the chain of command. But today's U.S. Army cannot afford to have any divisions "on ice," and this pressure would drive competence. Two such divisions is the irreducible initial number, since one urban combat division would be rapidly exhausted by the pace of deployments.

Most of the divisional artillery would be shifted to corps level, while engineers at all levels would be increased and restructured, including the addition of organic sapper platoons to infantry battalions. Composite armor and mechanized elements would be added to light forces at a ratio of one battalion (brigade) to four, with a longer-term goal of developing more appropriate and readily deployable means of delivering direct firepower and protecting the forward movement of troops. Innovative protection of general transport would be another goal. Military intelligence units would have to restructure radically and would need to develop habitual relationships with reserve-component linguists and area specialists. Aviation would work closely with other arms to develop more survivable tactics, and each division would gain an active-duty PSYOPS company. Signalers would need to experiment with low-cost, off-the-shelf tools for communicating in dense urban environments, and an overarching effort would need to be made to create interdisciplinary maps, both paper and electronic, that could better portray the complexity of urban warfare. The divisions' experience would determine future acquisition requirements.

But none of the measures cited above is as important as revolutionizing training for urban combat. The present approach, though worthwhile on its own terms, trains soldiers to fight in villages or small towns, not in cities. Building realistic "cities" in which to train would be prohibitively expensive. The answer is innovation. Why build that which already exists? In many of our own blighted cities, massive housing projects have become uninhabitable and industrial plants unusable. Yet they would be nearly ideal for combat-in-cities training. Although we could not engage in live-fire training (even if the locals do), we could experiment and train in virtually every other regard. Development costs would be a fraction of the price of building a "city" from scratch, and city and state governments would likely compete to gain a U.S. Army (and Marine) presence, since it would bring money, jobs, and development—as well as a measure of social discipline. A mutually beneficial relationship could help at least one of our worst-off cities, while offering the military a realistic training environment. The training center could be at least partially administered by the local National Guard to bind it to the community. We genuinely need a National Training Center for Urban Combat, and it cannot be another half measure. Such a facility would address the most glaring and dangerous gap in our otherwise superb military training program. We need to develop it soon.

An urbanizing world means combat in cities, whether we like it or not.

In summary, an urbanizing world means combat in cities, whether we like it or not. Any officer who states categorically that the U.S. Army will never let itself be drawn into urban warfare is indulging in wishful thinking. Urban combat is conceptually and practically different from other modes of warfare. Although mankind has engaged in urban combat from the sack of Troy to the siege of Sarajevo, Western militaries currently resist the practical, emotional, moral, and ethical challenges of city fighting. Additional contemporary players, such as the media and international and nongovernmental organizations, further complicate contemporary urban combat. We do not want to touch this problem. But we have no choice. The problem is already touching us, with skeletal, infected fingers. The U.S. military must stop preparing for its dream war and get down to the reality of the fractured and ugly world in which we live—a world that lives in cities. We must begin judicious restructuring for urban combat in order to gain both efficiency and maximum effectiveness—as well as to preserve the lives of our soldiers. We must equip, train, and fight innovatively. We must seize the future before the future seizes us.

The Future of
Armored Warfare

We miss our animals. Since history closed the mounted arm's stables, soldiers have compensated by naming their units after dragons, lions, panthers, and their great lost love, the horse. Tankers, especially, like to associate themselves with the sleek and ferocious. Unfortunately, the armored vehicles of the next century are apt to resemble hedgehogs, snakes, and caterpillars. Perhaps, someday, a hard-bitten NCO will slam down his beer mug, stand up, and declare, "I'm from the Woolly-Bears, mister, and we don't like that kind of talk."

Armored vehicles will be around for a long time to come. But their shapes, sizes, weights, armor, armaments, propulsion, connectivity, battlefield awareness, and crewing will change profoundly. The continuity will be in the mission: to deliver local killing power and allow protected maneuver. The evolution of armored vehicles will be driven by technology and strategic requirements, but above all by the changing environment of combat: the increasing urbanization of warfare, and the growing transparency of traditional nonurban operations—in which we will be able to monitor the activities of enemy forces in real time. Far from being the twilight of the tank, the new era could become a great age of armor, but only if proponents and practitioners of mounted combat are willing to engage the future in a spirit of honest inquiry.

The hints that Armor needs to reform itself grow ever harder to ignore. First, in the Gulf War, it took an infantryman to recognize that the ground battle had opened in the pursuit phase. Too many Armor commanders sought to fight textbook battles—and the textbooks were outdated editions that elevated secure flanks above knockout blows. Then came the Russian experience in Grozniy. Our reaction was to mock Russian incompetence and repeat the old saw that you don't send armor into cities. We failed to recognize the future, just as Europeans, content to assume American military incompetence, failed to appreciate the killing power of rifled weapons demonstrated in our Civil War. Half a century later, the Europeans reprised Cold Harbor on a vast scale on the Somme. Will we reenact the battle of Grozniy?

Yes, the Russians were militarily incompetent in Chechnya. But they had no choice other than to use armored vehicles in city streets—like all advanced armies, they lacked the infantry strength to reduce the city building by building. Between these two examples, our soldiers found themselves in deadly combat in Mogadishu under conditions that begged for armor. Apart from the political considerations that denied our troops the tools they needed to overwhelm their opponents, the military itself was guilty of relying on traditional approaches to urban operations that are no longer feasible when domestic elites panic in the face of casualties (friendly or enemy).

The lessons of these examples are many, but the core challenges come down to a few points. Mounted warfare in nonurban environments goes very fast, and will go faster. Traditional control measures are inadequate. Battlefields quickly become cellular and multidirectional, and therein lies more opportunity than danger for the force with informational superiority and a leadership unafraid of the initiative of subordinates. While rigorous training and equipment quality are essential, the key variable is situational awareness—both the practical kind that means seeing the enemy tank before it sees you, and the deeper sort of command visualization that allows a leader to understand not only the physical reality of the enemy situation but, more important, the situation as the enemy perceives it.

In the future, formations will operate far more swiftly and in smaller increments than in even the most successful divisional attacks during Desert Storm, but this is the reborn paradigm: go fast, hit the enemy's weaknesses, keep on hitting him, and don't stop moving. This is very old military wisdom. Somehow, somewhere between the National Training Center and Carlisle, many of us forgot it. Too often, we elevate safety of decision over decisiveness. We may admire Jackson, but we imitate McClellan.

The lessons of Chechnya are even more relevant than those of our incomplete victory on the banks of the Euphrates. In the lethal urban canyons of Grozniy—a rather small city, by world standards—the Russian military urgently needed means of protected fire and movement. They were forced to use what they had, and what they had was wrong. Equipment designed for war in the European countryside, flawed tactics, and grossly inadequate training and command and control led to disaster. The Russian experience does not prove that armor was the wrong answer, only that the Russians had the wrong kind of armor—and used that badly.

The key to the future of armored warfare lies in disregarding what we expect a tank to be in order to focus on what we need the tank of the future to do.

Tomorrow's Armored Force

On those disappearing battlefields that do not center on urban environments and complex terrain, tanks will remain recognizable for at least a generation. We will see changes in lethality, protection, propulsion, and weight, but the greatest advance will be in battlefield awareness. On-board, remote, and even strategic sensors will give our tankers a commanding view of the battlefield, and there will be a window of frustration as their vision outstrips their engagement range. Eventually, tanks will gain a much deeper indirect-fire capability, and sensing munitions will make an increasing proportion of land engagements resemble over-the-horizon naval warfare. These extraurban tanks will be lighter and will go faster. Miniaturization of components, from engines through communications gear to ammunition, will pace advances in armor to make systems more rapidly deployable. Eventually, the tank's primary "armor" may be electromagnetic or may otherwise take advantage of physical principles we are only beginning to exploit. We can imagine developments from "battles of conviction," in which opposing combat systems struggle to "convince" each other's electronics to enter vulnerable configurations, to weapons that literally stop opponents in their tracks by manipulating the local environment. Many experiments will fail, but some—possibly the most radical—will succeed.

Despite protection advances, crews will remain the most vulnerable link in the armored warfare system. This will be compounded by the proliferation of weapons of mass destruction. Eventually we will see a variant of remote-control tanks operated by displaced crews that remain well apart from the advance—perhaps as much as a continent away. Rather than merely requiring a private with a toggle switch, the complexity of decision making will probably call for at least a two-man "crew" (per shift) even for robotic tanks. Virtual-reality control environments will keep things lively. It is also possible that future tanks will be dual capability—normally directly crewed, but capable of remote operation under extreme threat conditions.

To complement the tanks, we will develop hyperprotective troop carriers to facilitate those dismounted activities indispensable to land warfare. But even here robotics will play a role, so that we can operate under conditions created by weapons of mass destruction without soldiers present (although a human battlefield presence will always remain desirable—and usually essential). We may have to rethink mounted operations in the out-years: remotely crewed vehicles can maneuver through intervening, high-threat terrain while soldiers are air-delivered to link-up points in or near populated areas or complex terrain we cannot ignore. Tangentially, we are likely to develop vehicles with a come-when-I-call robotic capability, as well as specially intelligent tanks and troop carriers and, further along, "self-healing" vehicles that can repair and even remold themselves in response to battle damage.

"Flying tanks" have long been objects of speculation, but it is likely that fuel logic and the psychophysical dynamics of battle will demand grounded systems for many years to come. Although attack helicopters already incorporate many of the characteristics previously imagined for flying tanks, we have found them a complement to, not yet a substitute for, armored vehicles. If we do work toward flying tanks—in the interests of systems economy—the more successful approach would probably be to ask how helicopters could change so that they could move, shoot, and survive on the ground. Aircraft are conceptually more mutable than ground systems, and if the flying tank proponents are right, this might become the backdoor means to change the parameters of armored warfare. A very real danger, however, is asking any system to do too many things, resulting in a system that does nothing especially well. Striking a proper balance between specificity of purpose and flexibility of application is a fundamental systems-design problem.

> *A very real danger is asking any system to do too many things, resulting in a system that does nothing especially well.*

The relationship between means of direct and indirect fire will also change. As noted earlier, tanks will acquire a longer-range precision capability. At the same time, aircraft and then orbital platforms will deliver an ever greater proportion of the firepower we apply to combat in open areas. Great advances are on the horizon for fire coordination, and we are likely to see simultaneous joint attacks on complex targets by tanks, satellites, and hunter-killer computers. As with the Armor branch, Field Artillery needs to break from means-centered models and focus on the required ends. The alternative is to decline into the role of niche player—too heavy to deploy rapidly, too clumsy for urban operations, and a nonplayer in the information battle. Although the goal of warfare will always be to destroy the enemy, the first step today is to inflict systems paralysis on conventional opponents, from air defense systems to command and control and, increasingly, to national information infrastructures. What will tomorrow's "artillery" look like?

We are becoming so powerful at traditional modes of warfare that we will drive our enemies into environments where our efficiency plummets, our effectiveness drops, and close combat remains the order of the day.

The long-term trend in open-area combat is toward overhead dominance by U.S. forces. Battlefield awareness may prove so complete, and precision weapons so widely available and effective, that enemy ground-based combat systems will not be able to survive on the deserts, plains, and fields that have seen so many of history's great battles. Our enemies will be forced into cities and other complex terrain, such as industrial developments and intercity sprawl, where our technical reconnaissance means cannot penetrate or adequately differentiate and our premier killing systems cannot operate as designed. We will become victims of our success. We are becoming so powerful at traditional modes of warfare that we will drive our enemies into environments where our efficiency plummets, our effectiveness drops, and close combat remains the order of the day. We will fight in cities, and we need tanks that can fight and survive in their streets.

The Changing Nature of Cities

Urban operations—the tanker's nightmare—will be the growth area for armored warfare. The world is becoming a network of cities with marginalized hinterlands. Increasingly, cities transcend statehood. In this contradictory world, where nationalism has returned in plague force, nation-states are softening. Cities as diverse as Vancouver, Frankfurt, Moscow, Miami, and Shanghai are growing apart from their parent states, for reasons that range from ethnic shifts in the population base to wealth concentration. Vancouver doesn't need the rest of Canada. Moscow doesn't much want the rest of Russia, except as an ornament of power and a looting ground. Shanghai may not be able to "afford" China indefinitely. Miami has become the shadow capital of Latin America—a focal point of information, culture, investment, banking, society, and exile. Frankfurt am Main is well on the way to becoming a German city with an ethnic German minority (and extensive districts of Berlin are populated exclusively by economic migrants).

An ancient paradigm is reversing: while cities long sucked strength from the diverse resources of the state, the state is increasingly becoming a parasite on the world's more successful cities. This shift does not apply to cities such as Washington, D.C., or Marseilles, which would collapse entirely without state support, but it is very much the case in boomtowns such as Hyderabad, Ho Chi Minh City, and Seattle. In the postmodern American model of dispersed cities, Silicon Valley has to foot the bill for failed governmental models in yesterday's cities, and every useful federal function performed in Washington, D.C., could be transferred profitably to northern Virginia or Maryland, were it not for habit and sentimentality. Suburbia is becoming "posturbia," and even in Ireland and Britain, the

industries of the future are moving toward capable populations, instead of expecting the hands and minds to relocate to
cities where the quality of life is abysmal. In this tiered construct, boom cities pay for failed states, postmodern dispersed
cities pay for failed cities, and failed cities turn into killing
grounds and reservoirs for humanity's surplus and discards
(guess where we will fight).

Human clustering has left behind the village (the primary
node of human organization until the middle of the twentieth
century, and humanity's moral arbiter) and is concentrating in
these three models: *boom cities* (Manhattan, Munich, Vancouver,
Seoul, Austin); *reservoir cities,* where humanity is held in suspen-
sion (Lagos, Johannesburg, Lima, Karachi, Calcutta, Los Angeles proper, Cairo); and *dispersed cities* (the greater Washington
area without the District of Columbia, Silicon Valley, the Los
Angeles region without the city of Los Angeles, Atlanta minus
its urban core). Of note, the dispersion of America's success
functions, with the transition of suburbia to a wonderfully liv-
able workplace, is as misunderstood as American culture—
decried by elitists, it creates the highest, healthiest, and most
desired standard of living in history—just as American culture
is the world's all-time best-seller, despite condescending
reviews. We're winning again.

We live in the most dynamic age in human history. The
city—capstone of human organization—is growing, changing,
producing fantastic wealth, and rotting. Although numerous
factors are involved, the primary catalyst of change is the information revolution. In this Age of Contradiction, the value of
information has inflated, and the cost of information has
plummeted. Information always generated power; today, it generates wealth at a breathless pace—and cities (including Amer-

ica's dispersed cities) are humanity's information banks. If we possessed the data to calculate an "information deposit coefficient" for the populations of cities such as the greater Boston area (winner) and Bombay (loser), we would probably be astonished at the per capita informational advantage in Boston. Compounding the problem, the information that is available in the world's loser cities is not only scarce but generally inaccurate, episodic, and deformed by local prejudice.

While many cities and post-cities are growing richer, more powerful, and more efficient, others—especially in societies with information disorders—are becoming poorer (on a per capita basis), weaker in their ability to self-regulate, and unable to deliver the most basic services that allow human beings to coexist in great densities. Many of these reservoir cities are anarchies attenuated by apathy, and the apathy of the masses can transform itself very quickly into violence. We are entering a period when we will increasingly judge the success of cities and their environs before we concern ourselves with their moldering states. This will not be a global model, however. Countries such as the United States (for all our urban problems) manage to maintain a symbiotic dynamism between city and countryside, bridged by "third way" development: those dispersed cities coalescing from culturally chaste suburbs, satellite enclaves of production, and the workload diffusion characteristic of information mastery. Foreign actors will have to contend with the United States, not just Los Angeles, for the rest of our lifetimes.

But who cares about upper Egypt if Cairo is calm? We do not deal with Indonesia—we deal with Jakarta. In our evacuation of foreigners from Sierra Leone, Freetown was all that mattered. For decades, we dealt not with the government of

Zaire but with the emperor of Kinshasa, and in the recent civil war in that vast African state (now renamed as yet another Congo), military progress was measured not in jungle traversed but in cities conquered. India is well on the way to becoming a confederation of city-states disguised as a political unity. Hong Kong will be a fascinating laboratory for the relative power of the city versus the state.

There is no global village. The village is dying as a model, and it is dead as a source of power. Instead, a global network of cities and post-cities is emerging, of both the healthy and the faltering, whose elites interact across borders more efficiently and effectively than they interact with the populations of their own hinterlands. Our elites will be inclined to defend foreign elites, even at the expense of our own population (this is already the paradigm of U.S.-Mexican and U.S.-Saudi relations). Our future military expeditions will increasingly defend our foreign investments rather than defending against foreign invasions. And we will fight to subdue anarchy and the violent "isms" because disorder is bad for business. All this activity will focus on cities.

In the future, the term "urban warfare" will become a redundancy.

New Armor for Urban Warfare

Where does armor fit in? Today's armor, designed for a war that—blessedly—never was, is ill designed for urban combat. Yet until better designs reach our soldiers, we will need to make do with what we have. Ideally, that would lead to reassessments of our tactics and reorganization of our units. We have begun to accept the inevitability of urban operations, but the truth is that we are likely to resist significant preparations until a sizable number of our service members have been killed and our nation embarrassed. That is the price we pay for any military paradigm shift following a period of successful organizational performance: the world may have changed, but we won't "mess with success." At a time when the pace of technological and social change is without precedent in human history, our military is clinging to the past. We are behaving like a blue-collar union in a smokestack industry.

> *At a time when the pace of technological and social change is without precedent in human history, our military is clinging to the past. We are behaving like a blue-collar union in a smokestack industry.*

We can affect the out-years, though. If you catch decision makers on a good day, they *can* be persuaded to sign up for changes that will not begin to remold the force on their watch. We have a free conceptual environment for anything beyond a decade, and we need to take advantage of it by asking ourselves practical questions about the future employment of armor in urban environments: What do we need that armor to do? How would we like it to do it? What are the extremes of the possible?

Regarding firepower, armor for urban environments will need two types of guns—or one gun that can do a variety of jobs. We will need a crude blasting capability, and we will need maneuverable munitions that can follow an assigned target beyond the limits of pure ballistic trajectories. We need old-fashioned flechette-type munitions—or an innovative substitute—and we need rounds that can penetrate multiple layers of steel and concrete before exploding or otherwise "blooming" a follow-on destructive capability. "Boomerang" weapons that respond instantly to attack and track the assailant until he or it is eliminated would be an especially powerful deterrent. We will need a counterelectronics capability and crowd-control "weaponry." It is important not to limit conceptualizing to traditional guns; an ammunition-free technique that achieves the desired effect could become part of our weapons suite. Any means we develop to isolate portions of the urban battlefield would offer a tremendous advantage. Again, it is essential to focus on the task, not the known means for performing that task.

But the primary job of armored vehicles in urban areas will be to protect maneuver, movement, and resupply. Because urban environments promise endless ambushes, we need new forms of armored protection—not just layers of steel or laminate or ceramics, or even reactive armor as it presently exists. Tomorrow's layers of armor will begin with spoofing techniques that complicate target detection on the part of enemy systems, before proceeding to environmental or atmospheric modification capabilities that defeat mines, distort the enemy's perceptions, and disrupt the trajectory and integrity of enemy munitions. Instead of today's rigid hulls and turrets, tomorrow's armor may be malleable, capable of reshaping itself in response to changing threat environments. Self-repair and, in the following generation, self-healing of battle damage are logical goals. Finally, "living" armor, with its principles based on biological models, may allow new levels of interaction among man, machine, and environment.

Armored vehicles for urban warfare must also be nimble. Although long-range sustained speeds are not a requirement, a sprint capability is essential. The vehicles must be highly maneuverable—at least in some variants. Deployment requirements and the varieties of urban operations suggest a modular approach, either to total armored fighting systems or at least to troop carriers. The ability to "task organize" vehicle size, power units, armaments, electronic warfare (EW) suites, and battlefield awareness capability is worth pursuing. Vehicles that could operate as compact individual entities or join together to form moving fortresses or to "circle the wagons" would offer new flexibility. Armored "mother ships" could "feed" or harbor smaller vehicles and robotic devices. Robotic scouts might climb through rubble, navigate corridors, or explore sewers, followed by team carriers with human decision makers and actors. These would be backed up by caterpillar mini-fortresses that hustle through streets and possess not only offensive and defensive environmental controls but also segmentation and self-repair capabilities. The visual signatures of our armored systems, to the extent we do not obscure them, should be composed to psychologically disarm the enemy, exploiting research on instinctive reactions to shapes, colors, sounds, and smells. Our systems should be sensually terrifying to opponents and intimidating to populations.

Urban warfare is three-dimensional. Armored vehicles, using drones or ground robotics or hypersensors, must be able not only to see into multistory structures and down into sewers, subways, and service tunnels but also to introduce soldiers—in a protected manner—to upper-story or subterranean zones of operation. Ideally, armored vehicles would be able to caterpillar above or snake below ground level, gripping the lower portions of structures or entering subterranean passageways. This might be done with deployed subcomponents, such as team-capsule vehicles, or with extensions from master vehicles. The ability to cross exposed "ground" will be essential. A well-designed vehicle or extension might seal against a second-story window, "sanitize" the immediate interior, and release soldiers from an armored gate. To some extent, the soldier himself might become an armored entity.

Secured areas might be outposted by robotics and picketed by soldiers cued by local fusion centers that combine intelligence from sources as diverse as miniature roaming sensors and national-level systems. Population control might be established by electronically registering every inhabitant with whom the force comes in contact and alerting in response to any human concentrations that do not fit habitation profiles. Eventually, body signature sensors should identify fear, hostility, or positive demeanors on the part of the locals. Any means that can be developed to separate the hostile actor from the sea of people is highly desirable, since, in urban operations, the enemy's ultimate camouflage is his humanity.

A model urban operation of the future might begin with a massive information operations effort that attacks not only systems but also souls. Air and space forces would then isolate the city electronically and through fires, attack preselected targets with precision munitions, suppress air defenses, and impose barriers between urban subsectors. Army robotics parachute in to secure airfields and landing zones, followed by air-delivered troops with light armored vehicles to extend the perimeter. The next wave includes heavier ground systems and more personnel delivered by air and, in littoral cities, by Navy-Marine operations. Robotic systems push deeper into the urban area, followed by armored reconnaissance "moving fortresses" or combinations of separate vehicles, delivering firepower and dismountable forces to hostile zones. Behind the fighters, military police and intelligence personnel process the inhabitants, electronically reading their attitudes toward the intervention and cataloging them into a database immediately recoverable by every fire team in the city (even individual weapons might be able to read personal signatures, firing immediately upon cueing).

Wherever the enemy resists, joint operations isolate and reduce the threat zone. Smart munitions track enemy systems and profiled individuals. EW actions veil the movement of armored vehicles, remotely exploding mines as the vehicles move forward. Tanks and tank segments deliver direct and smart fires in a final barrage as troop carriers advance. The unit commander designates points of entry, and images of exteriors and interior layouts appear in the carriers for orientation. Carriers leech against buildings and subterranean passage entry points, collapsing the atmosphere at the points of entry to kill or disable any present enemies before discharging troops. In extremely vertical environments, robotics and troops are air-delivered by systems that can spoof enemy sensors and vision into registering multiple images or completely false images. As soldiers clear the buildings—preceded by their individual sensors—they push their individual weapon's selector switch to "Inhabited," and upon entering a room, the weapon does not discharge if pointed at a noncombatant without violent intent. Most friendly casualties are lost to enemy suicide attacks or come as the result of physical injuries received during fire and movement within buildings, such as broken limbs. When particularly stiff pockets of resistance develop, smart armor moves in to destroy them, or soldiers cue stand-off precision weapons.

Other armored units move swiftly through the city to establish a mobile presence and seize control of line-of-communication nodes and routes of ingress to and egress from the city. In vast conurbations, lightweight, electronically armored systems are airlifted by rotary-wing (or post-rotary-wing) assets. Satellites monitor the city for any air defense fires, cueing immediate responses from near-space orbiting "guns." Drones track processed inhabitants who have been "read" as potentially hostile and "tagged." Any suspect concentrations draw immediate intervention. Nonlethal weapons control crowds and manage POWs. Operations continue twenty-four hours a day until the city is cleared of hostiles. When the environment is deemed acceptably safe, United Nations peacekeepers arrive to conduct the long-term operations necessary to restore or create an acceptable government and civil functions. U.S. intelligence and electronic support continues, but U.S. troops return to the United States or to forward bases to prepare for subsequent expeditionary actions.

Many of the hypotheses contained in this essay will never be realized—not because they are too far fetched, but because they will prove inadequately imaginative. We will develop far more appropriate, incisive, and interesting solutions than those offered here. Yet even if every avenue of development proposed here is wrongheaded, the urban operations challenge is real, immediate, and growing. We *will* fight in cities. Even when we are not fighting, we will operate in urban areas and in complex terrain on a variety of missions. The development of radically imagined means for armored warfare in urban terrain will be essential for the beginning of the new millennium.

What guidelines will help us to accomplish urban (or other) missions successfully? In future operations, whether in

1999 or 2029, the U.S. military should strive to follow tenets such as these:

1. Extract a clear mission statement from decision makers.

2. Tell the American people that there will be friendly casualties.

3. Establish unity of command and purpose.

4. Impose rules of engagement that favor U.S. forces, not the enemy.

5. Deploy more combat power than you think you need, then increase it.

6. Operate offensively, never passively or defensively, and operate continuously.

7. Never allow local inhabitants to congregate en masse.

8. Do the job fast. If the job can't be done fast, get somebody else to do it.

9. Hand off the pacified city to non-U.S. peacekeepers as soon as possible.

10. From first to last, fight and win the information war— on all fronts.

The physical contours of warfare have changed dramatically in our time, and they will continue to evolve. Thinking about the problem is a first step. The next step is to begin to prepare our remarkable military for reality.

A Revolution
in Military Ethics?

There is a popular disposition to regard ethics as absolute and enduring, yet they are neither. That which is considered ethical alters with time and varies among civilizations and even families. At some impalpable level, the impulse to ethics does appear to arise from within and may be a collective survival strategy conditioned by biological and cultural evolution. Yet the specific content of a civilization's or a society's ethics is generally determined by accumulative tradition, epochal convenience, and local habit. The ethics of war and conflict are especially fluid.

We live in a stage of Western civilization in which nameless casualties inflicted by bombing campaigns are acceptable, while the thought of summarily shooting a prisoner of war fills us with revulsion, even if the blood of war crimes drips from every finger of that prisoner. We are allowed to impose embargoes that strike the most powerless members of foreign populations, bringing deprivation, malnutrition, and deformity to the voiceless, while merely annoying antagonistic decision makers. Yet we must treat foreign entrepreneurs who torment our poor with narcotics as white-collar criminals entitled to the legal protections of our own Constitution. Where is the absolute ethical quality, or even the logic, of this unexamined behavior? Our military and foreign policy ethics have the nature of a great historical chain letter that warns but does not reward.

Ethics are enablers. Personal, social, or military, they allow us to interact without needless viciousness and without generalized violence to the soul, the body, or society. In the military sphere, ethics in war allow us to disguise psychologically the requirement to butcher other human beings, masking the blunt killing behind concepts such as just war, higher causes, and approved behaviors. Ethics in war on the part of a Western society do not so much protect the objects of our violence as they shield us from the verity of our actions. Military ethics are ceremonial in the religious sense: they codify the darkness, implying a comforting order in the chaos and void. So long as we believe that we have behaved ethically, we can, statistically, bear the knowledge of our deeds.

In our time, much of the debate over what is and is not ethical military behavior has focused on the overarching issue of just and unjust wars. But we rarely examine the component parts of our ethical stance, even when, as in the Allied bombing campaigns of the Second World War, technological capability proved so enticing that it canceled ethical restraints that had prevailed in Europe for over two and a half centuries, since the armies of Louis XIV ravished the Rhenish Palatinate. Overall, the greatest cause of perversion in the "logic" of military ethics has been the rise of technologies that distance the killer from the killed, impersonalizing warfare and thus dehumanizing this archetypal male group activity. When English longbowmen struck down masses of French knights with early stand-off precision weapons, chivalry reacted with a horror that we can no longer grasp. Crécy and Agincourt marked a profound civilizational change from biological to technological logic. Warfare was no longer a contest of individual qualities played out in groups, but a contest of mass against mass, with the man subordinated to the mechanism. While this enabled the rise of disciplined armies as we know them, it also offset war from any individual biological imperative.

Gunpowder weapons furthered this trend dramatically until, today, only snipers and hapless "peacekeepers" consistently get a detailed look at their enemies. The enemy has become faceless, and easier than ever to kill. The unexpected consequence of the advent of distancing weapons, however, has been that we in the West find it ever more distasteful to dispose of those enemies who acquire faces and, thus, identities. The celebratory combat of the *Iliad* survives only in the sports contests that have always been a substitute and preparation for biologically competitive warfare. Our wars are, or attempt to be, wars of alienation.

Modern man has dehumanized warfare.

The "Highway of Death" issue in the closing phase of Desert Storm is a good example. Although the decision makers in Washington, shy of consequences since Vietnam, feared a reaction of disgust on the part of the American electorate, most Americans were justifiably proud of the performance of their military (after having been warned by countless journalists and disanalytical scholars that their country's weapons did not work and their kids could not fight). The man in the street—or in front of the television set—had no qualms about killing countless Iraqis in that pristine Nintendo war. The citizenry of the

United States, in fact, will tolerate the killing of enormous numbers of foreigners, so long as that killing does not take too long, victory is clear-cut, friendly casualties are comparatively low, and the enemy dead do not have names, faces, and families. Our bombing campaign that prepared the battlefield for the ground attack buried countless Iraqi conscripts alive in sandy trenches and bunkers, while killing and wounding tens of thousands more in less dramatic fashion. The conscripts by and large did not want to be there, but feared their own leaders and military gendarmerie, and bore little or no direct responsibility for Iraqi excesses in Kuwait City. We killed those who did not have the courage to desert. Yet killing them in their thousands was "legitimate" and untroubling. Try slapping one prisoner on CNN.

> *The citizenry of the United States, in fact, will tolerate the killing of enormous numbers of foreigners, so long as that killing does not take too long, victory is clear-cut, friendly casualties are comparatively low, and the enemy dead do not have names, faces, and families.*

Our most recent campaign in the desert highlighted another ethical disconnect: whereas it was acceptable to bomb those divisions of hapless conscripts, it was unthinkable to announce and carry out a threat to kill Saddam Hussein, although he bore overwhelming guilt for the entire war and its atrocities. We justify this moral and practical muddle by stating that we do not sanction assassination in general, and certainly not the assassination of foreign heads of state. Yet where is the ethical logic in this? Why is it acceptable to slaughter—and I use that word advisedly—the commanded masses but not to mortally punish the guiltiest individual, the commander, a man stained with the blood of his own people as well as that of his neighbors?

Legalists—and reflexive moralists—will warn that a policy that sponsors assassinations or supremely focused military strikes could degenerate into a license to murder that would corrupt our institutions and our being. First, that is symptomatic of our Western tendency to view all things in black and white, as either-or. Killing a Saddam, and doing it very publicly, does not mean that we would then wipe out the cabinet of every foreign government that ran late on its debt repayments. We are capable of judicious selectivity.

More important, though, is our willful blindness to issues of guilt, relative guilt, and guiltlessness. Objectively viewed, our position is perverse and cruel when we allow great criminals to escape punishment while attacking their subject populations, infrastructure, or simply their military establishments. Let me be clear: as a soldier, I do not object to assisting in the battlefield killing of as many foreign opponents as it takes to accomplish the mission assigned by my commander in chief. As a human being, however, our "ethical" national behavior reminds me of those feudal squabbles in which minor nobles dueled by killing and raping each other's serfs and burning unoffending villages.

At its present stage of historical development, it is very difficult for the United States (or for most other Western nations) to engage in an unjust war. Our dilemma is that of defining just and unjust actions within our wars and conflicts. It is time to reexamine habits that have come to pass for ethics and ask the sort of questions that are as controversial as they are uncomfortable to the man or woman of conscience.

One subject, touched on above, that merits separate study is the extent to which technology determines our acceptance of behaviors as legitimate or not. It appears that technology is the greatest of temptations in this sphere of human activity; what is unacceptable from the man is welcome from the machine. If the soldier shoots a family, he is a war criminal. If a pilot misses his target and wipes out a family, he has simply had an unsuccessful mission. The focus is not on the result, but on the distance between the actor and the object of his actions, on the alienation between subject and object. Since the pilot "could not have known" and presumably did not will the result of his actions, he bears no guilt. The machine failed, and the machine is guilty (although the machine's designers bear no blame, so long as they have designed machines that are linear extrapolations of previous war machines and they do not explore weaponry that violates contemporary—or atavistic— taboos, such as chemical or biological weapons).

The high-performance aircraft is at once an extension of the rifle and qualitatively different from it. The rifle dehumanized individual combat to a degree, but beyond-visual-range systems obliterate the human factor. Sophisticated technological systems with stand-off capabilities are perceived as the real killing mechanisms, not their operators. We speak of soldiers entering a town but of aircraft—not pilots—flying above it. Much is permitted to the machine that is forbidden to the man. It is an enormous ethical failure, yet one that, at least until now, has enabled us to win conventional wars.

The practical difficulty today lies in the range of unconventional conflicts, from peacekeeping operations to punitive expeditions by any other name. The close-in nature of combat in these conflicts insists on rehumanizing an activity we believed we had successfully dehumanized. In the streets and alleys of Mogadishu, the divide between subject and object collapses, and the alienation is cultural, not physical. This cripples our ability to fight.

The ethical restrictions on our military organizations function well enough in combat against other militaries, but increasingly our enemies, our potential adversaries, and even our regional partners either do not know or reject our Western ethics (at times they do not even adhere to the ethics of their own society or civilization, since some cultures find mass ethics fungible, although collective taboos are not). We face opponents, from warlords to druglords, who operate in environments of tremendous moral freedom, unconstrained by laws, internationally recognized treaties, and "civilized" customs, or by the approved behaviors of the international military brotherhood. These men defeat us. Terrorists who rejected our worldview defeated us in Lebanon. "General" Aideed, an ethical primitive by our standards (and probably by any standards), defeated us in Somalia. Despite occasional arrests, druglords defeat us on a daily basis. And Saddam, careless of his own people, denied us the fruits of our battlefield victory. In Bosnia and on its borders, intransigents continue to hold our troops hostage to a meandering policy. Our enemies play the long game, while we play jailbird chess—never thinking more than one move ahead. Add in the readiness of these enemies to spend their human capital freely, and the only way we see out of our dilemma (we're here, we're ineffectual, now what?) is to go home with the local situation unchanged, if not worsened by our efforts.

Until we change the rules, until we stop attacking foreign masses to punish by proxy protected-status murderers, we will continue to lose. And even as we lose, our cherished ethics do not stand up to hardheaded examination. We have become not only losers but random murderers, willing to kill several hundred Somalis in a single day but unwilling to kill the chief assassin, willing to uproot the coca fields of struggling peasants but without the stomach to retaliate meaningfully against the druglords who savage our children and our society.

We *must* reexamine our concepts of the ethical and the legal. The oft-lauded Revolution in Military Affairs is consistently associated with technological capability, but a genuine revolution in military affairs, one that would upset the trend of history and shift the nature of war, would be a military doctrine, recognized by government, that stated that the primary goal of any U.S. war or intervention would be to eliminate the offending leadership, its supporting cliques, and their enabling infrastructure. If our technological capabilities enjoy such great potential, why not focus research and development on means we can use against enemy leaders and their paladins? Why continue to grind within the antique paradigm that insists that the leader is identical with his (or her) people and, therefore, punishing the people or their military representation is a just response to the leader's offenses?

In antique ages—probably spiritually healthier—the aim of war between states or proto-state organizations was to kill the enemy chief or to capture him and display him in a cage. Entire peoples often suffered, but they were not usually the primary targets, and their suffering was often an incidental result of the lack on either side of the technological wherewithal to bound past intervening armies and populations to reach the ranking offender and his immediate circle. You had to cut your way through the mass to reach The Man. Then, with the rise of Western civilization, leaders realized that it was not a profitable precedent to hurt each other's persons, and personal combat and direct physical vengeance between leaders disappeared on our sliver of the planet—and later, as we projected our ways, elsewhere. Rulers and leaders distanced themselves from the hazards of combat and fought by proxy with armies, then, in our century, with populations. Why not, for the first time in modern history, refocus military operations on punishing the truly guilty? In the twentieth century, we would have liked to strike Hitler directly, but did not have the means. So we destroyed the cultural treasure-house that was Dresden out of spite.

Current and impending technologies could permit us to reinvent warfare—to once again attack the instigators of violence and atrocity, not the representational populations who themselves have often been victimized by their leadership. The whispered warning that we do not condone "assassinations" because we do not want our own leaders assassinated is a counsel of unspeakable cowardice. First, if leaders will not risk the fate they ask of their privates, they are not fit to lead their people. Second, if foreign criminals, official or private, knew that retribution would be generally swift and always sure, attacks on U.S. leaders—or U.S. citizens overall—would likely decrease wonderfully. And such a policy would return us once again to an objectively moral path. Our current system amounts to punishing the murderer's neighborhood, while letting the murderer go free.

This is not a prescription for ending conventional war or mass conflict. The dirty secret is that many human beings like to fight, and so long as demagogues can transfer the responsi-bility for personal and collective failure onto foreign or other-wise different groups, we will have to respond to mass violence, and that will sometimes require a violent response against the mass. But this is not an all-or-nothing world. We could revolu-tionize—and humanize—military activity by attacking the sources of evil directly and minimizing, when possible, assaults against those faceless foreign masses. If we only forced our-selves to stop and think, who among us would not be better sat-isfied with Saddam Hussein dead than with the ghosts of twenty or thirty thousand or more common Iraqis rising from the sands of Kuwait and southern Iraq?

And what do we expect or want of our shrunken military establishment? Haven't we forced ourselves through a thresh-old requiring dramatically different strategies and doctrine? Wouldn't a doctrine of the focused pursuit of guilty individuals and their immediate accomplices make more sense for our jew-eler's military of today? Must we content ourselves with doc-trine still heavy with the legacy of the massive assembly-line militaries we enjoyed when technology was affordable in bulk and military service was a broadly accepted responsibility?

It is time to rehumanize warfare.

And old divisions of labor do not hold. Since the long-com-fortable lines between military and law-enforcement missions are collapsing in our fractured world, we must treat the most murderous foreign criminals who attack our citizens as military targets. Currently, our drug control policy, at home and abroad, concentrates overwhelmingly on controlling and punishing those at the bottom of the narcotics business. We must recognize that foreign criminals who attack the most vulnerable segments of our citizenry, bringing death to our streets and disorder to our polity, have no entitlement to U.S. constitutional protection. The primary difference between Saddam Hussein and the druglords of Colombia or Mexico is that Saddam Hussein never attacked the United States or its population directly.

These issues demand serious debate. Traditionalists who decry even the possibility of attacking these sources of human misery in such a manner generally do so from campuses or comfortable offices. They are out of contact with our citizenry and its needs, as they are phenomenally out of contact with the sheer violence of this world. They will immediately push the issue to absurd extremes, crying out that such a doctrine would amount to giving our military a license to kill. *But the purpose of a military is to kill, and if you cannot stomach that, you should not have a military.* The only operative question is *whom* the military should kill. More important, it would not be left to sergeants or, in most cases, even to generals to decide which foreign leaders or criminals should die or be otherwise punished. That would be the task of our elected and appointed leaders, or their delegated representatives, as it always has been.

> *The purpose of a military is to kill, and if you cannot stomach that, you should not have a military.*

Even though Hitler never attacked the United States, we saw a need to go to war against Germany—not merely to admonish Hitler in policy journals for disturbing the peace. We justified shooting the most vital man in Japan, Admiral Yamamoto, out of the sky. And we executed the most-deserving German and Japanese war criminals after perfunctory trials.

We *can* muster the will to strike evil at its source, and we must not continue to succumb to the allure of attacking faceless populations when such actions are no longer a technological necessity. Today, we increasingly have the means to execute atrocious leaders and criminal mass murderers without fire-bombing Tokyo or Hamburg. We have the means to prevent wars and conflicts, or to stop them in their earliest stages, by aiming our military directly at the responsible parties. Do we not also have the duty to do so?

The United States enjoys a historically unique position of power, influence, and cultural empire. Whether we find this crown comfortable or not, we bear unprecedented responsibilities—and face unanticipated vulnerabilities. If we truly will protect our citizens, our allies, and peace (that most anomalous condition of mankind), it is time to stand back and reevaluate our conception of what is ethical in war and in those haunting almost-wars arising from foreign disorder and international organized crime. We might discover that our current military ethics are the least humane thing about us.

Blood-isms

Not long ago, with communism coughing up its diseased lungs, radical Islamic fundamentalism seemed the obvious candidate to provide the West with a galvanizing threat. Although politically correct intellectuals were initially a bit disoriented by the notion that indigenous forces in the stagnant areas of the world might be less than virtuous, the repeated brutalities of fundamentalists from Iran to Sudan so bloodied the fairy tales about the psychology of underdevelopment that it became acceptable to oppose—circumspectly—the "excesses" of fundamentalism. God's men in Teheran slaughtered Baha'is and communists with equal fervor, savagely repressed political dissent, shackled the media, tossed their countrywomen back into the Dark Ages, and refused to compromise on anything ever. Fundamentalists deepened the ineffably stupid Lebanese civil war, rolled back social progress in Pakistan, and went on a blood-soaked rampage in "almost European" Algeria. They blew up airliners and killed tourists. They poked pocketknives into charred American corpses and took hostages. Then they danced in the streets, fired their rifles into the air, and yelled at us. Not only were they unashamed, they seemed to be having an astonishingly good time. We had found our new bad guys.

Then came Yugoslavia. Nagorno-Karabakh. Moldova. Ossetia. Abkhazia. Chechnya. An epidemic of virulent xenophobia erupted, from the Baltic states down through the Balkans: a black new beginning, not the end of something. The ending was the death of neo-Leninist hegemony and the Soviet empire. What we see now is the brave new world.

Even within the fortress of the Russian Federation, tiny peoples whose homelands Western experts cannot pinpoint on a map demanded independence from Moscow. Reason as a political force played no role. Ethnic groups of 100,000 or so— little more than extended families—cried out for their own governments and flags. Nationalism, against which our century's great wars had supposedly inoculated us, came back with a power over the human soul that is simply not comprehensible to the educated U.S. citizen (although, even within the United States, a nativist fringe in Hawaii calls for secession).

Fundamentalism, which to Americans, after all, is primarily a bother to foreigners, has fallen to second place on the roll of threats to Western well-being (although it still figures powerfully). The horrendous images and reports from Yugoslavia— so recently the exemplary darling of intellectuals (and where the people look a bit more like us)—drove home the revised lesson: the real number-one threat of the future is nationalism, and nationalism is now the domain where academics and government analysts can make careers.

As always, we are reacting to the crisis—or crises—of the moment. We never thought the fundamentalist problem through. Conditioned sociopolitical inhibitions may make it even more difficult to understand what nationalism is about, since it not only thumbs its nose at an incredibly wide range of cherished disciplines, from sociology to political science, but also discredits virtually every cola commercial produced in the last thirty years. We are not going to teach the world to sing by handing it a sweet little bottle of tolerance. The world is too busy shrieking. And those indigenous peoples who were supposed to teach us humanity, the nobility of poverty, and how to be one with nature are having a grand time killing their neighbors, mass raping the women from the next village, blasting and burning out the homes and history of anyone born on the other side of the ridge or across the river, and threatening to explode dams, chemical plants, and nuclear reactors.

Is nationalism, then, the critical factor with which we must cope?

Or does fundamentalism remain the ultimately greater menace, despite the transitory, if bloody, dynamics at play in the wreckage of empires?

Must we now prepare to fight a two-front ideology-inspired war?

The answer to each question is no, on technical grounds.

Nationalism and fundamentalism are not separate problems. They are essentially identical. If their rhetoric differs, their causal impulses do not. Their psychological appeal to the masses is identical. Nationalism is simply secular fundamentalism. To the extent they differ at all, religious fundamentalism may even become the preferable disease from the U.S. standpoint. In any case, these are *twin* enemies. And we are going to have to struggle with them, on many fields, for a very long time to come.

How could all those people in the intriguing folk costumes let us down like this? We planned our vacations to admire them, we made charitable contributions to give them a helping hand, we praised them lavishly when they took their first baby steps toward the sort of behavior we valued. They were such charming waiters, and it was fun to go shopping in the bazaar. To prove our earnestness, we helped them study in our universities and even let them open restaurants in our cities, where we could drink terrible wine and reminisce about our holidays. Materially speaking, they were making progress.

Nationalism and fundamentalism are not separate problems. They are essentially identical. . . . Nationalism is simply secular fundamentalism.

We've been through all this, of course. We are conversant with the idea of "perceived relative deprivation," the observation that societies slip into crisis when expectations exceed the possibilities of fulfillment, no matter the objective measure of progress. But even this basically sound insight understates the sheer vanity of humankind.

Every major religion warns its adherents of the danger of vanity, decrying the sin of pride or insisting that only humility can lead to enlightenment. In our rush from religion—be that flight good or bad—we have certainly lost this fundamental insight. Everyone everywhere wants more, usually in the most vulgar material sense, because the display of possessions seems to verify the worth of the self—"I have, therefore I am." We announce ourselves to our peers through the possession of the mutually desired object. And while European intellectuals, caught in a pathetic time warp, rail against American materialism, the importance of "signifying" possessions is far greater in economically stagnant or developing states. In Moscow, home-grown entrepreneurs in top-of-the-line Mercedes speed by the newly impoverished. For an Iranian, possession of a foreign-made VCR is a far greater mark of distinction than possession of a locally printed Koran. Within the United States, the most baldly materialistic social sector is composed of young males from the inner cities, with their ritual gold chain jewelry and their willingness to risk prison if not their lives to acquire an expensive car or at least an ornate pair of athletic shoes. These young people fit a classic Third World rejectionist model—they know what they want and believe they deserve, but they are impatient with the legitimate means of acquiring it.

This cult of sheer material possession as a substitute for practical accomplishment is one of the most severe childhood diseases of civilization—it stunted the growth of Islamic culture just as it has, more recently, incalculably retarded the develop-ment of functioning economies in sub-Saharan Africa and, to a lesser extent, in Latin America. Any culture or subculture where possession has been disassociated from positive contrib-utory accomplishment degenerates into social cannibalism This is as true of the U.S. welfare class as it was of the propri-etary culture of the Spanish Empire in America or as it is of the oil-rich lands of the Persian Gulf. Much of the world has simply disassociated the concept of "having" from that of "earning," whereas the recognition of the need to earn—either God's grace or an improvement in the individual's material lot—was a motive force in the rise of the West.

The collision with foreign modernity has brought most non-Western cultures the worst of both worlds: they retain the vanity impulse, even experience it in an intoxicatingly aggra-vated form, while imagining that they can skip entirely the difficult process that has legitimized the possession of "signify-ing" objects in Euro-America. Our own good-hearted intellec-tual corruption compounds the problem whenever we apologetically agree with a failing nation or continent as it cries out that the West has no right to the wealth it has earned. Too often, those of us most sincerely concerned with foreign suffer-ing simply reinforce utterly groundless assumptions that aggra-vate the plight of the object of pity. Europeans—and Japanese and other successful Asians—did not always have computers in their homes and CAT-scan equipment in every hospital. If any-thing, resource-deprived Europe (and, again, Japan) had to come from behind in the race for well-being. Now we are the adulated model (until disillusionment sets in—see below), and the world's failures, both individuals and entire cultures, don't much like it.

The emergence of enduring liberal democracies in a small corner of the world is probably the most complex cosmic acci-dent of the past millennium. Expecting violently different cul-tures to adopt the finery of liberal democracy and wear it with panache is as silly as expecting Guinea-Bissau to compete with Silicon Valley in the technological sphere. Rather than enter-ing a new golden age of liberal democracy, we may find that other cultures are beginning to fall farther away from our stan-dard, just as the lower echelons of the Third World continue to fall farther behind the West in both absolute and relative mea-sures of modernity.

While hybrid democracies may function in Latin America or India because they have been adapted to suit regional, pop-ular, and elite vanities, we may find that democracy's high-water mark has already been reached elsewhere: the echoes we hear mark its melancholy retreat or, at best, its deformation.

What are the common denominators of nationalism and fundamentalism?

• Both are born of a sense of collective failure that frees the individual from responsibility for personal failure. Nationalism and fundamentalism then transfer the blame for the collective failure to another culture, religion, or ethnic group or, initially, to internal opponents. Thus, the individual has failed only because his party was driven to failure by a malevolent external force. Shouts of "Death to America" or ethnic battle cries in the Balkans punctuate the efforts of broken men and failed cultures to become whole again.

• There is always a sense of historical grievance. This may be real, exaggerated, or imaginary. It does not necessarily involve the contemporary opponent, but deepens and solemnizes the sense of national or religious martyrdom.

• Both preach a lost golden age that can be resurrected only when the nation is purged of corrupting foreign influences. Interestingly, although fundamentalism reinforces this golden-age myth with promises of a gorgeous hereafter, no significant fundamentalist movement has omitted the vision of an earthly paradise lost and to be regained.

• Both dehumanize their opponents and view mercy toward enemies as an irresponsible show of weakness. The corollary to this is that both preach the inherent superiority of their kind, whether ethnic, religious, or a combination of the two.

• Both are dynamically violent. Nationalist and fundamentalist leaders come to power on two-track platforms of rebirth and revenge. They can excuse purges, severe economic sacrifice, bloody battlefield stalemates, and even comprehensive failure, but they cannot excuse inaction; their adherents want change, even if it proves cataclysmic. One of the rare differences is that fundamentalism can longer content itself with the persecution of domestic enemies—heretics real and imagined—while nationalism generally carries with it the spirochete of irredentism, of tribal unification, of enosis.

• Both are aggravated by exposure to Euro-America. Not so long ago, this exposure was limited to diplomats, adventurers of miraculous variety, and the occasional thin red line drawn up at the foot of a hill. Today, Euro-America—especially the United States—is everywhere, thanks to the proliferation of media technology. But far from serving the causes of education and understanding, mass media have become the world's single greatest cause of cultural disorientation. We provide ill-chosen information to people unprepared to process it and thus elicit shock, revulsion, and jealousy, along with pathetic attempts at emulation, whose failure leads to embitterment.

> *Far from serving the causes of education and understanding, mass media have become the world's single greatest cause of cultural disorientation.*

We have yet to grasp the crisis of values that arises when an insular, traditional culture is flooded by images of another culture that is vastly more successful materially but whose values are antithetical to those cherished by the receptor society.

Initially, the young and capable often imagine that by aping externals they can transcend the differences and attain the level of (various forms of) wealth, comfort, and convenience of the external society. The two primary forms of this imitation of the external model are *domestic*, in which the subject seeks to "import" the lifestyle he desires, and *émigré,* in which the subject travels to the promised land. The domestic approach may lead to material well-being in lucky cases, but it fractures the society. The émigré model can work for those willing to assimilate to the necessary degree, who have a talent for mimicry, and who are doers. But it also produces fundamentalist and nationalist leaders through a process of *multiple alienations.* First, the subject becomes alienated from his own "backward" society; however, unable to satisfy his vanity in the adopted "progressive" society, he undergoes a second alienation and concludes that the superior virtues lay slumbering in the religion or ethnic culture he abandoned. He assumes the mission of reshaping his roots to meet a higher, exclusive standard, accenting differences, not commonalities, with the foreign culture that betrayed him. He runs home to an idealized mommy. Or, to use a more mature metaphor, the psychology parallels that of a man who leaves his wife for an intoxicating other woman, only to be ultimately rebuffed. He feels betrayed and seeks revenge; meanwhile, his abandoned wife is idealized as the embodiment of virtue, whether or not this corresponds to objective reality.

The greatest failures among Third World émigrés are consistently intellectuals and the children of established families (often one and the same person) who do not find the automatic, unqualified recognition in the object culture that they enjoyed at home. Even if they attain professorships or manage to buy lives of great mortal comfort, they tend to remain outsiders, also-rans. These are the men who go home to start (often reactionary and always xenophobic) revolutions that reject the foreign culture that rejected them. Wounded vanity has motivated cross-cultural problem children from Arminius,

who recognized a Roman glass ceiling when he struck it with
his Germanic head, to Ho Chi Minh, who had to work as a
scullery knave in Paris; from Clausewitz, who learned to hate
France during his captivity as a prisoner of war, to a recent
prime minister of Greece, whose academic career in California
proved ultimately dissatisfying to the Balkan bully lurking
under the tweeds.

It is impossible to satisfy the vanity of intellectuals, and the
collision of intellectuals from the failing regions of the world
with the ultimately exclusive cultural context of the West profoundly aggravates their ever-wounded pride. And, thanks to
modern means of communication, they don't even have to leave
the farm to find out they're hicks. That is why we are so often
shocked to find that bloody-minded nationalist leaders such as
Karadzic or Gamsakhurdia were respected intellectual and cultural figures back home: poets, historians, doctors, professors.

So much of the progress imagined for the postcolonial era
has come to nothing. All that remains to failing nations and
cultures is the ceaseless assault of things foreign, dazzling, and
humiliatingly unattainable.

---

*So much of the progress imagined for the
postcolonial era has come to nothing. All that
remains to failing nations and cultures is the
ceaseless assault of things foreign, dazzling, and
humiliatingly unattainable.*

Western popular media are immeasurably more powerful
in their impact on the values of other cultures than on our
own. Wailing that television and popular music play havoc

with the morals of our youth, we become obsessed by the behavior of the marginalized elements of our society, while most kids grow up as normally as they ever did. Because our children receive the media in a greater environmental context, most learn intuitively to filter reality from fantasy to a workable degree. The impact that we should worry about strikes foreign cultures that have not acquired a discriminating mechanism from their social context and therefore cannot adequately separate fact from fiction. Gang movies may cause a temporary increase in minority-on-minority violence outside theaters in U.S. cities—since segments of our urban youth also lack this discriminating mechanism to some degree—but Arnold Schwarzenegger films do not cause statistically significant eruptions of mass slaughter in Middle America. An American ten-year-old knows intuitively that movies are an illusion. Many foreign adults do not. I have personally met numerous would-be Rambos in Armenia and Georgia, even in Moscow, and the grisly clowns driving the war in what was Yugoslavia were enraptured by film images. Yet Croatians, Serbs, Russians, Georgians, and Armenians have long-standing ties to Western culture. Imagine the effect on those who have no frame of reference whatsoever.

In 1992 I caught a rattling airliner from Yerevan to Moscow. The aged Aeroflot jumbo wore a new Armenian flag on its tail, and the cabin was crowded with travelers, many of them refugees, sitting on broken-backed seats or huddling in the aisles. It was almost impossible to move about, given the mounds of shabby luggage that had been brought aboard, and the flight attendants disappeared after takeoff, not to be seen again. All in all, it seemed like a typical domestic flight over the corpse of the USSR. And then they caught me off guard: they

showed an in-flight movie, something unthinkable on the old
Aeroflot domestic runs.

This nod to competitiveness and world custom was a bit
marred, however, by the film chosen. It was a black-and-white,
English-language, ultra-cheap "dungeons and dragons" affair,
with unknown players and a startling mix of cold steel violence
and nudity—some of which involved imaginitive perversions.

Some of the travelers were well connected and relatively
sophisticated; others were low-level entrepreneurs off to trade
all they could carry in Moscow markets. Many were refugees
from the sputtering, thug-fueled war in the mountains—
refugees for whom Yerevan had no more resources and who
hoped to rescue themselves with distant relatives or just a vague
address in Moscow. Some of these people had never been on
an aircraft before, and many of them certainly had not seen a
film of this sort. But suddenly, there it was: the West.

The men—all of them—watched with passionate interest as
huge swords descended and packs of deformed creatures fon-
dled a demi-heroine's naked breasts. Sometimes a phenomenally muscled hero saved the girl in a rush of violence,
sometimes not (it was, all in all, a rather existential affair).
Invariably, an explicit coupling followed the bursts of violence.

The female passengers, Christian in religion but oriental
in conditioning, theatrically averted their eyes. Then they
hungrily scouted the more shocking bits from their trenches
of decorum.

Personally, I found the movie repulsive and dumb. It was
pitched at the pimpled twelve-year-olds whom R and X ratings
were created to attract. But even a Western twelve-year-
old would clearly perceive this as fantasy. The film was, however,
perfectly tempered to inspire the absolute worst behavior in the

sort of credulous and infantile adult males who are presently slaughtering each other in the Caucasus and elsewhere.

A final note on the unrecognized power of the entertainment media: no contemporary fundamentalist movement, Islamic or otherwise, has attacked the West on grounds of profound religious difference (although they don't mind massacring sects they view as heretical). The complaints, from Western religious zealots and Iranian theocrats, have consistently been directed against *secular* influences (Mark Twain, women's rights, and other horrors). They attack not religious beliefs but encroaching cultural contexts. Neither nationalists nor fundamentalists fear alternative beliefs, religious or secular. They fear dissident *behavior*, since behavior (certainly not art) is the ultimate manifestation of culture. And the most accessible—and therefore insidious—examples of this frightening behavior are provided by the entertainment media. In their appreciation of the threat posed by the proliferation of audio and video technology, the mullahs and reactionaries in the failing regions of the world are far ahead of Western academics, with their quaint, pathetic love of books (the recorded voice cassette is perhaps the most effective propaganda tool employed by Islamic militants). The "battle of behavior" has nothing to do with ideas. It has to do with images—short skirts, not long theories—and with the seductiveness of pop hits that will not leave the ear. The threat doesn't come from Harvard. It comes from Hollywood.

Perhaps the greatest fallacy (out of so many) in contemporary Western diplomatic belief is the conviction that we can more readily reason with and trust in nationalists than fundamentalists. In fact, the matter is purely situational, and it may at times be preferable to lie down with the fundamentalist cat (when we must) than the nationalist dog. We might, on a good and lucky day, get up with fewer fleas.

The behavior of Islamic fundamentalists in power has generally been deplorable. They torture without remorse, imprison or execute without trial, and restrict basic freedoms to a degree intolerable to Westerners. Yet, after all the gore has been hosed into the sewer, there is a moral center to the greatest of the fundamentalists. It just isn't our moral center. Not many fundamentalist leaders share our taste for liberal democracy (which we acquired over the better part of a millennium), but some do share other ideals we profess. The best of the fundamentalists are resolutely against the corruption that has so enervated the failing regions of the world. They are for mass education (although we might not agree with the curriculum and their exclusion of women). They desire to democratize the nation's wealth, if not its government. They seek to do that which socialist demagogues only promised. They have a sense of honor higher than that prevalent in the deathbed societies they seek to revitalize. And their actions have yet to prove anywhere near as belligerent toward other states as their rhetoric.

Nationalists, in contrast, tend to have a moral center smaller and softer than the inside of a Tootsie Roll Pop. Hitler was a nationalist. Mussolini was a nationalist. The military leadership that steered Japan down the road to Hiroshima was rabidly nationalist. Even Stalin, despite his Georgian antecedents, became a Russian nationalist. Enver Pasha, the butcher of Armenians, was a nationalist, and Mao ultimately proved more nationalist than communist. Today, all the creepy little ex-party bosses with Elvis haircuts who sponsor ethnic cleansing or the suppression of minority rights from Dushanbe to the Danube are nationalists—even when they profess otherwise for reasons of expedience or intellectual confusion. Nationalists have not been good to our century, and it does not appear that they will be much kinder to the next.

Samuel Johnson, normally a precise fellow with his language, misspoke on one fateful occasion, declaring, "Patriotism is the last refuge of the scoundrel." He meant to say, "Nationalism is the last refuge of the scoundrel." He just didn't have the vocabulary.

Despite the relative virtues of fundamentalism as currently practiced and promised vis-à-vis nationalism, there is, in the end, not much pleasure in the choice between them. By their essential nature, both nationalism and fundamentalism stand firmly against "us." We are the necessary Satan, the galvanizing enemy.

If fundamentalism is sometimes marginally less repulsive than nationalism, it is, unfortunately, less able and willing to cooperate or compromise with the West. Fundamentalism is utterly rejectionist, while nationalism is only partially so. Nationalists are more mentally agile—and less scrupulous— and can more easily digest sophisticated techniques and technologies that promise them advantage. Nationalists are also far more flexible when it comes to rationalizing alliances. Finally, nationalists are quicker to welcome foreign assistance, particularly if it is humiliating, threatening, or best of all, lethal to their neighbors.

But the problems in dealing with nationalists and fundamentalists, whether fighting them or aiding them, are virtually identical:

• If you enter an alliance with them, you must support them without reservation, no matter how heinous their deeds. The moment you introduce moral scruples concerning treatment of the enemy or begin to speak of compromise and just settlements, you have betrayed them and you will become their enemy.

• Both will interpret any offer of a just peace from an enemy as a sign of that enemy's weakness.

• Neither fundamentalists nor nationalists will honor any form of agreement a moment longer than it suits their needs—unless they are afraid to abrogate it.

• Even when they admire your practical prowess, you are despised as a lesser creature.

• Both are dogmatic and thus will behave even more irrationally than other states.

• Both will inevitably commit atrocities that will embarrass any Western state allied with them. In peacetime, they will commit domestic atrocities; in wartime, they will mistreat enemy soldiers and the enemy population.

• In war, they will employ all available means to win, no matter the degree of moral censure they receive, unless they clearly understand that they will be punished for their behavior by an external force so powerful that even the most obstinate fundamentalist or nationalist ruler must recognize his relative impotence. Even then, some of them will ignore the danger of penalties.

• Not all nationalists or fundamentalists will fight to the last man, but their behavior cannot be confidently predicted in advance, and it will vary from culture to culture. Without exception, the best way to make war against them is to deliver an initial blow so comprehensive and powerful that it emasculates them militarily and psychologically. Even then, the true believers among them may continue to resist.

• As stated above, nationalists and fundamentalists need enemies. Although nationalists are more apt to carry this *Feindbild* over into active aggression against another state, the quickest way to start or expand a war of aggression by nationalists or fundamentalists is to let them imagine that they have your unequivocal support, or that you need theirs.

• No matter the extent of your support or the sincerity of your commitment to nationalists or fundamentalists, it will never be viewed as sufficient.

• You will always be suspect.

• Your interests don't count.

Where nationalist and fundamentalist currents exist in the same nation, they are (perhaps increasingly) symbiotic. Even nationalists who harbor no personal religious beliefs find that traditional religions lend credibility to the nationalist cause—as well as expanding its power base. Conversely, fundamentalist movements, such as the one in Iran, can broaden their acceptance by couching harsh programs in terms of national necessity. This symbiosis thrives in the ruins of Yugoslavia. Prior to the outbreak of the wars of dissolution, religious differences in Yugoslavia pretty much meant that the population failed to go to the church or mosque of its choice. Bosnian Muslims were perhaps the least religious of any major Muslim population. The Serbian Orthodox Church slumped on the shoulders of bent old women, and Croatian Roman Catholics were perhaps more European in their disregard of religion than in any other respect. Yet members of each side in that guilt-rich conflict wrapped themselves in the armor of a true faith overnight, perceiving nearly defunct religious professions as a perfectly good reason to butcher and rape neighbors who resembled them genetically, behaviorally, and materially.

To an extent, the rediscovery of traditional religion by ethnic groups fired with the nationalist impulse is natural, since religion is an important part of any people's history. Religious establishments, for their part, welcome growth opportunities and official protection. Even in countries not ruptured by civil war, populations and governments often have a difficult time determining the proper relationship between religion and nation. Poland is discovering that the church triumphant is not entirely without imperfections, while governmental actors in Turkey are assuredly playing with fire when they entertain Islamic fundamentalists and endanger the unique legacy of Ataturk. Saddam Hussein tried—with limited success, thanks to his sordid past—to play the Islamic card during the Gulf War, while nationalist leaders in India and Pakistan have long recognized the power of appealing to religion whenever party energy threatens to flag. It is impossible to separate religion from nationalism in Israel, and the preservation of Islam's sanctity is perceived by some to be the only moral justification for Saudi statehood.

In an age haunted by cataclysms real and imagined, in this era of disappointment and wracking international failure, men and women will prove increasingly vulnerable to antimodern, antirational explanations for their misfortunes and their inextinguishable impulse to vanity. Even in the United States, many of those least able to keep material, intellectual, and spiritual pace with the demands of modernity turn to primitive or exotic religious forms, from revivalism to New Age God-candy. In the failing regions of the world, such trends can only acquire greater momentum. There are no irreversible physics in the fundamentalism-to-nationalism equation: unsatisfying nationalism can evolve "backward" into theocracy. To update the most thoughtful soldier who ever learned to write, "Nationalism is merely the continuation of fundamentalism by other means."

Our century has been one of fragmentation, of devolution that flirts with chaos. Mankind has not experienced so universal a breakdown in the established political order since the shattering of the Roman Empire. Brotherhood-of-man platitudes have been consigned to the "ash heap of history" with even greater certainty than has Marxism-Leninism, but we, convinced of the all-conquering virtue of liberal democracy, still cannot accept the essential realities of human political behavior. The world has cancer, and we are in the denial phase. If you want to see the future, look to Cambodia, to Somalia, to "Kurdistan," or to Yugoslavia, Angola, Tajikistan, or Georgia.

We Americans must avoid fantastic schemes to rescue those for whom we bear no responsibility, and we must resist imagining a moral splendor for murderers who better understand media manipulation than the murderers with whom they are in conflict. We must learn not to trust our eyes and ears—and especially their electronic extensions. The media, forever focusing on the crisis of the moment, almost never understand what they witness. In dealing with nationalism and fundamentalism, we must be willing to let the flames burn themselves out whenever we are not in danger of catching fire ourselves. If we want to avoid needless, thankless deaths among our own countrymen, we must try to learn to watch others die with equanimity.

We won't learn this, of course. We will be moved to action because of our emotional needs, heightened by the nonsense of postcolonial guilt. We will send troops to places where they can do no long-term good. We will be forced to choose which human beasts to back. And we will always pay more than we expected to pay when we began our intervention.

Constant Conflict

We have entered an age of constant conflict. Information is at once our core commodity and the most destabilizing factor of our time. Until now, history has been a quest to acquire information; today, the challenge lies in managing information. Those of us who can sort, digest, synthesize, and apply relevant knowledge soar—professionally, financially, politically, militarily, and socially. We, the winners, are a minority.

For the world masses, devastated by information they cannot manage or effectively interpret, life is "nasty, brutish, and short-circuited." The general pace of change is overwhelming, and information is both the motor and the signifier of change. Those humans, in every country and region, who cannot understand the new world, or who cannot profit from its uncertainties, or who cannot reconcile themselves to its dynamics will become the violent enemies of their inadequate governments, of their more fortunate neighbors, and ultimately of the United States. We are entering a new American century in which we will become still wealthier, culturally more lethal, and increasingly powerful. We will excite hatreds without precedent.

We live in an age of multiple truths. He who warns of the "clash of civilizations" is incontestably right; simultaneously, we shall see higher levels of constructive trafficking between civilizations than ever before. The future is bright—and it is also very dark. More men and women will enjoy health and prosperity than ever before, yet more will live in poverty or tumult, if only because of the ferocity of demographics. There will be more democracy—that deft liberal form of imperialism—and greater popular refusal of democracy. One of the defining bifurcations of the future will be the conflict between information masters and information victims.

We are entering a new American century in which we will become still wealthier, culturally more lethal, and increasingly powerful. We will excite hatreds without precedent.

In the past, information empowerment was largely a matter of insider and outsider, as elementary as the division of society into the literate and the illiterate. Although superior information—often embodied in military technology—has killed throughout history, its effects tended to be politically decisive but not personally intrusive (once the raping and pillaging were done). Technology was more apt to batter down the city gates than to change the nature of the city. The rise of the modern West broke the pattern. Whether speaking of the dispossessions and dislocations caused in Europe through the introduction of machine-driven production or those caused elsewhere by the great age of European imperialism, an explosion of disorienting information intruded ever further into Braudel's "structures of everyday life." Historically, ignorance was bliss. Today, ignorance is no longer possible, only error.

The contemporary expansion of available information is immeasurable, uncontainable, and destructive to individuals and entire cultures unable to master it. The radical fundamentalists—the bomber in Jerusalem or Oklahoma City, the moral terrorist on the Right, or the dictatorial multiculturalist on the Left—are all brothers and sisters, all threatened by change, terrified of the future, and alienated by information they cannot reconcile with their lives or ambitions. They ache to return to a golden age that never existed, or to create a paradise of their own restrictive design. They no longer understand the world, and their fear is volatile.

Information destroys traditional jobs and traditional cultures; it seduces, betrays, yet remains invulnerable. How can you counterattack the information others have turned upon you? There is no effective option other than competitive performance. For those individuals and cultures that cannot join or compete with our information empire, there is only inevitable failure (of note, the Internet is to the techno-capable disaffected what the United Nations is to marginal states: it offers the illusion of empowerment and community). The attempt of the Iranian mullahs to secede from modernity has failed, although a turbaned corpse still stumbles about the neighborhood. Information, from the Internet to rock videos, will not be contained, and fundamentalism cannot control its children. Our victims volunteer.

These noncompetitive cultures, such as that of Arabo-Persian Islam or the rejectionist segment of our own population, are enraged. Their cultures are under assault; their cherished values have proven dysfunctional, and the successful move on without them. The laid-off blue-collar worker in America and the Taliban militiaman in Afghanistan are brothers in suffering.

It is a truism that throughout much of the twentieth century the income gap between top and bottom narrowed, whether we speak of individuals, countries, or in some cases continents. Further, individuals or countries could "make it" on sheer muscle power and the will to apply it. You could work harder than your neighbor and win in the marketplace. There was a rough justice in it, and it offered near-ecumenical hope. That model is dead. Today, there is a growing excess of muscle power in an age of labor-saving machines and methods. In our own country, we have seen blue-collar unions move from center stage to near irrelevance. The trend will not reverse. At the same time, expectations have increased dramatically. There is a global sense of promises broken, of lies told. Individuals on much of the planet believe that they have played by the rules laid down for them (in the breech, they often have not), only to find that some indefinite power has changed those rules overnight. The American who graduated from high school in the 1960s expected a good job that would allow his family security and reasonably increasing prosperity. For many such Americans, the world has collapsed, even as the media tease them with images of an ever-richer, brighter, fun world from which they are excluded. These *discarded citizens* sense that their government is no longer about them, but only about the privileged. Some seek the solace of explicit religion. Most remain law-abiding, hardworking citizens. Some do not.

The foreign twin is the Islamic or the sub-Saharan African or the Mexican university graduate who faces a teetering government, joblessness, exclusion from the profits of the corruption distorting his society, marriage in poverty or the impossibility of marriage, and a deluge of information telling him (exaggeratedly and dishonestly) how well the West lives. In this age of television-series franchising, videos, and satellite dishes, this young, embittered male gets his skewed view of us from reruns of *Dynasty* and *Dallas,* or from satellite links beaming down *Baywatch,* sources we dismiss too quickly as laughable and unworthy of serious consideration as factors influencing world affairs. But their effect is destructive beyond the power of words to describe. Hollywood goes where Harvard never penetrated, and the foreigner, unable to touch the reality of America, is touched by America's irresponsible fantasies of itself; he sees a devilishly enchanting, bluntly sexual, terrifying world from which he is excluded, a world of wealth he can judge only in terms of his own poverty.

Most citizens of the globe are not economists; they perceive wealth as inelastic, its possession a zero-sum game. If decadent America (as seen on the screen) is so fabulously rich, it can only be because America has looted one's own impoverished group or country or region. Adding to the cognitive dissonance, the *discarded foreigner* cannot square the perceived moral corruption of America—a travesty of all he has been told to value—with America's enduring punitive power. How could a nation whose women are "all harlots" stage Desert Storm? It is an offense to God, and there must be a demonic answer, a substance of conspiracies and oppression in which his own secular, disappointing elite is complicit. This discarded foreigner's desire may be to attack the "Great Satan America," but America is far away (for now), so he acts violently in his own neighborhood. He will accept no personal guilt for his failure, nor can he bear the possibility that his culture "doesn't work." The blame lies ever elsewhere. The cult of victimization is becoming a universal phenomenon, and it is a source of dynamic hatreds.

It is fashionable among world intellectual elites to decry "American culture," with our domestic critics among the loudest in complaint. But traditional intellectual elites are of shrinking relevance, replaced by cognitive-practical elites—figures such as Bill Gates, Steven Spielberg, Madonna, or our most successful politicians—human beings who can recognize or create popular appetites, recreating themselves as necessary. Contemporary American culture is the most powerful in history, and the most destructive of competitor cultures. Although some other cultures, such as those of East Asia, appear strong enough to survive the onslaught by adaptive behaviors, most are not. The genius, the secret weapon, of American culture is the essence that the elites despise: ours is the first genuine people's culture. It stresses comfort and convenience—ease—and it generates pleasure for the masses. We are Karl Marx's dream, and his nightmare.

Secular and religious revolutionaries in our century have made the identical mistake, imagining that the workers of the world or the faithful just can't wait to go home at night to study Marx or the Koran. Well, Joe Sixpack, Ivan Tipichni, and Ali Quat would rather study *Baywatch*. America has figured it out, and we are brilliant at operationalizing our knowledge. Our cultural power will hinder even those cultures we do not undermine. There is no "peer competitor" in the cultural (or military) department. Our cultural empire has the addicted—men and women everywhere—clamoring for more. And they pay for the privilege of their disillusionment.

American culture is criticized for its impermanence, its "disposable" products. But therein lies its strength. All previous cultures sought ideal achievement that, once reached, might endure in static perfection. American culture is not about the end but the means, the dynamic process that creates, destroys, and creates anew. If our works are transient, then so are life's greatest gifts—passion, beauty, the quality of light on a winter afternoon, even life itself. American culture is *alive.*

This vividness, this vitality, is reflected in our military; we do not expect to achieve ultimate solutions, only constant improvement. All previous cultures, general and military, have sought to achieve an ideal form of life and then fix it in cement. Americans, in and out of uniform, have always embraced change (though many individuals have not, and their conservatism has acted as a healthy brake on our national excesses). American culture is the culture of the unafraid.

Ours is also the first culture that aims to include rather than exclude. The films most despised by the intellectual elite—those that feature extreme violence and to-the-victors-the-spoils sex—are our most popular cultural weapon, bought or bootlegged nearly everywhere. American action films, often in dreadful copies, are available from the Upper Amazon to Mandalay. They are even more popular than our music, because they are easier to understand. The action films of Stallone or Schwarzenegger or Chuck Norris rely on visual narratives that do not require dialogue for a basic understanding. They deal at the level of universal myth, of pre-text, celebrating the most fundamental impulses (although we have yet to produce a film as violent and cruel as the *Iliad)*. They feature a hero, a villain, a woman to be defended or won, and violence and sex. Complain until doomsday; it sells. The enduring popularity abroad of the shopworn *Rambo* series tells us far more about humanity than does a library full of scholarly analysis.

When we speak of a global information revolution, the effect of video images is more immediate and intense than that of computers. Image trumps text in the mass psyche, and computers remain a textual outgrowth, demanding high-order skills: computers demarcate the domain of the privileged. We use technology to expand our wealth, power, and opportunities. The rest get high on pop culture. If religion is the opium of the people, video is their crack cocaine. When *we* and *they* collide, they shock us with violence, but statistically, we win.

As more and more human beings are overwhelmed by information, or dispossessed by the effects of information-based technologies, there will be more violence. Information victims will often see no other resort. As work becomes more cerebral, those who fail to find a place will respond by rejecting reason. We will see countries and continents divide between rich and poor in a reversal of twentieth-century economic trends. Developing countries will not be able to depend on physical production industries, because there will always be another country willing to work cheaper. The have-nots will hate and strive to attack the haves. And we in the United States will continue to be perceived as the ultimate haves. States will struggle for advantage or revenge as their societies boil. Beyond traditional crime, terrorism will be the most common form of violence, but transnational criminality, civil strife, secessions, border conflicts, and conventional wars will continue to plague the world, albeit with the "lesser" conflicts statistically dominant. In defense of its interests, its citizens, its allies, or its clients, the United States will be required to intervene in some of these contests. We will win militarily whenever we have the guts for it.

There will be no peace. At any given moment for the rest of our lifetimes, there will be multiple conflicts in mutating forms around the globe. Violent conflict will dominate the headlines, but cultural and economic struggles will be steadier and ultimately more decisive. The de facto role of the U.S. armed forces will be to keep the world safe for our economy and open to our cultural assault. To those ends, we will do a fair amount of killing.

> *There will be no peace. At any given moment for the rest of our lifetimes, there will be multiple conflicts in mutating forms around the globe.*

We are building an information-based military to do that killing. There will still be plenty of muscle power required, but much of our military art will consist in knowing more about the enemy than he knows about himself, manipulating data for effectiveness and efficiency, and denying similar advantages to our opponents. This will involve a good bit of technology, but the relevant systems will not be the budget vampires, such as manned bombers and attack submarines, that we continue to buy through inertia, emotional attachment, and the lobbying power of the defense industry. Our most important technologies will be those that support soldiers and Marines on the ground, that facilitate command decisions, and that enable us to kill accurately and survive amid clutter (such as multidimensional urban battlefields). The only imaginable use for most of our submarine fleet will be to strip out the weapons, dock them tight, and turn the boats into low-income housing. There will be no justification for billion-dollar bombers at all.

For a generation, and probably much longer, we will face no military peer competitor. Our enemies will challenge us by other means. The violent actors we encounter often will be small, hostile parties possessed of unexpected, incisive capabilities or simply of a stunning will to violence (or both). Renegade elites, not foreign fleets, should worry us. The urbanization of the global landscape is a greater threat to our operations than any extant or foreseeable military system. We will not deal with wars of Realpolitik, but with conflicts spawned of collective emotions, substate interests, and systemic collapse. Hatred, jealousy, and greed—emotions rather than strategy—will set the terms of the struggles.

We will survive and win any conflict short of a cataclysmic use of weapons of mass destruction. But the constant conflicts in which we selectively intervene will be as miserable as any other form of warfare for the soldiers and Marines engaged. The bayonet will still be relevant; however, informational superiority incisively employed should both sharpen that bayonet and permit us to defeat some—but never all—of our enemies outside of bayonet range. Our informational advantage over every other country and culture will be so enormous that our greatest battlefield challenge will be harnessing its power. Our potential national weakness will be the failure to maintain the moral and raw physical strength to thrust that bayonet into an enemy's heart.

Pilots and skippers, as well as defense executives, demand threat models that portray country X or Y as overtaking the military capability of the United States in ten to twenty years. Forget it. Our military power is culturally based. They cannot rival us without becoming us. Wise competitors will not even attempt to defeat us on our terms; rather, they will seek to shift the playing field away from military confrontations or turn to terrorism and nontraditional forms of assault on our national integrity. Only the foolish will fight fair.

The threat models stitched together from dead parts to convince Congress that the Russians are only taking a deep breath or that the Chinese are only a few miles off the coast of California uniformly assume that while foreign powers make all the right decisions, analyze every trend correctly, and continue to achieve higher and higher economic growth rates, the United States will take a nap. On the contrary. Beyond the Beltway, the United States is wide awake and leading a second "postindustrial" revolution that will make the original industrial revolution that climaxed the great age of imperialism look like a rehearsal by amateurs. Only the United States has the synthetic ability, the supportive laws, and the cultural agility to remain at the cutting edge of wealth creation.

Not long ago, the Russians were going to overtake us. Then it was oil-wealthy Arabs, then the Japanese. One prize-winning economist even calculated that fuddy-duddy Europe would dominate the next century (a sure prescription for boredom, were it true). Now the Chinese are our nemesis. No doubt our industrial-strength Cassandras will soon find a reason to fear the Galapagos. In the meantime, the average American can look forward to a longer life span, a secure retirement, and free membership in the most triumphant culture in history. For the majority of our citizens, our vulgar, near-chaotic, marvelous culture is the greatest engine of positive change in history.

Freedom works.

In the military sphere, it will be impossible to rival or even approach the capabilities of our information-based force because it is so profoundly an outgrowth of our culture. Our information-based Army will employ many marvelous tools, but the core of the force will still be the soldier, not the machine, and our soldiers will have skills that other cultures will be unable to replicate. Intelligence analysts, fleeing human complexity, like to project enemy capabilities based on the systems that a potential opponent might acquire. But buying or building stuff is not enough. It didn't work for Saddam Hussein, and it won't work for Beijing.

The complex human-machine interface developing in the U.S. military will be impossible to duplicate abroad, because no other state will be able to come from behind to equal the informational dexterity of our officers and soldiers. For all the complaints—in many respects justified—about our public school systems, the holistic and synergistic nature of education in our society and culture is imparting to tomorrow's soldiers and Marines a second-nature grasp of technology and the ability to sort and assimilate vast amounts of competitive data that no other population will achieve. The informational dexterity of our average middle-class kids is terrifying to anyone born before 1970. Our computer kids function at a level that foreign elites barely manage, and this has as much to do with television commercials, CD-ROMs, and grotesque video games as it does with the classroom. We are outgrowing our nineteenth-century model education system as surely as we have outgrown the manned bomber. In the meantime, our children are undergoing a process of Darwinian selection in coping with the information deluge that is drowning many of their parents. These kids are going to make mean techno-warriors. We just have to make sure they can do push-ups, too.

There is a useful German expression, *"Die Lage war immer so ernst,"* that translates very freely as *"the sky has always been falling."* Despite our relish of fears and complaints, we live in the most powerful, robust culture on earth. Its discontinuities and contradictions are often its strengths. We are incapable of five-year plans, and it is a saving grace. Our fluidity, in consumption, in technology, and on the battlefield, is a strength that our nearest competitors cannot approach. We move very fast. At our military best, we become Nathan Bedford Forrest riding a microchip. But when we insist on buying into extended procurement contracts for unaffordable, neotraditional weapon systems, we squander our brilliant flexibility. Today, we are locking in already obsolescent defense purchases that will not begin to rise to the human capabilities of tomorrow's service members. In 2015 and beyond, we will be receiving systems into our inventory that will be no more relevant than Sherman tanks and prop-driven bombers would be today. We are not providing for tomorrow's military, we are paralyzing it. We will have the most humanly agile force on earth, and we are doing our best to shut it inside a technological straitjacket.

There is no "big threat" out there. There's none on the horizon, either. Instead of preparing for the battle of Midway, we need to focus on the constant conflicts of richly varying description that will challenge us—and kill us—at home and abroad. There are plenty of threats, but the beloved dinosaurs are dead.

We will outcreate, outproduce and, when need be, outfight the rest of the world. We can outthink them, too. But our military must not embark on the twenty-first century clinging to twentieth-century models. Our national appetite for information and our sophistication in handling it will enable us to outlast and outperform *all* hierarchical cultures, information-controlling societies, and rejectionist states. The skills necessary to this newest information age can be acquired only beginning in childhood and in complete immersion. Societies that fear or otherwise cannot manage the free flow of information simply will not be competitive. They might master the technological wherewithal to watch the videos, but we will be writing the scripts, producing them, and collecting the royalties. Our creativity is devastating. If we insist on a "proven" approach to military affairs, we will be throwing away our greatest national advantage.

We need to make sure that our information-based military is based on the right information.

Facing this environment of constant conflict amid information proliferation, the military response has been to coin a new catchphrase—information warfare—and then duck. Although there has been plenty of chatter about information warfare, most of it has been as helpful and incisive as a discussion of sex among junior high school boys; everybody wants to pose, but nobody has a clue. We have hemorrhaged defense dollars to contractors perfectly willing to tell us what we already knew. Studies study other studies. For now, we have decided that information warfare is a matter of technology, which is akin to believing that your stereo system is more important to music than the musicians.

Fear not. We are already masters of information warfare, and we will get around to defining it eventually. Let the scholars fuss. When it comes to our military technology (and *all* technology is military technology), the Russians can't produce it, the Arabs can't afford it, and no one can steal it fast enough to make a difference. Our great bogeyman, China, is achieving remarkable growth rates because the Chinese belatedly entered the industrial revolution with a billion-plus popula-

tion. Without a culture-shattering reappreciation of the role of
free information in a society, China will peak well below our
level of achievement.

Yes, foreign cultures are reasserting their threatened identities—usually with marginal, if any, success—and yes, they are
attempting to escape our influence. But American culture is
infectious, a plague of pleasure, and you don't have to die of it
to be hindered or crippled in your integrity or competitiveness.
The very struggle of other cultures to resist American cultural
intrusion fatefully diverts their energies from the pursuit of the
future. We should not fear the advent of fundamentalist or
rejectionist regimes. They are simply guaranteeing their people's failure, while further increasing our relative strength.

> *We should not fear the advent of fundamentalist*
> *or rejectionist regimes. They are simply*
> *guaranteeing their people's failure, while further*
> *increasing our relative strength.*

It remains difficult, of course, for military leaders to con-
ceive of warfare, informational or otherwise, in such broad
terms. But Hollywood is "preparing the battlefield," and bur-
gers precede bullets. The flag follows trade. Despite our decla-
ration of defeat in the face of battlefield victory in Mogadishu,
the image of U.S. power and the U.S. military around the
world is not only a deterrent but also a psychological warfare
tool that is constantly at work in the minds of real or potential
opponents. Saddam swaggered, but the image of the U.S. military crippled the Iraqi army in the field, doing more to soften
them up for our ground assault than did tossing bombs into

the sand. Everybody is afraid of us. They really believe that we can do all the stuff in the movies. If the Trojans "saw" Athena guiding the Greeks in battle, then the Iraqis saw Luke Skywalker precede McCaffrey's tanks. Our unconscious alliance of culture with killing power is a combat multiplier that no government, including our own, could design or afford. We are magic. And we're going to keep it that way

Within our formal military, we have been moving into information warfare for decades. Our attitude toward data acquisition and, especially, data dissemination within the force has broken with global military tradition, in which empowering information was reserved for the upper echelons. Although our military is vertically responsible, as it must be, it is informationally democratic. Our ability to decentralize information and appropriate decision-making authority is a revolutionary breakthrough (the overpraised pre-1945 Germans decentralized some tactical decision making, but only within carefully regulated guidelines—and they could not enable the process with sufficient information dissemination).

No military establishment has ever placed such trust in lieutenants, sergeants, and privates, nor are our touted future competitors likely to do so. In fact, there has been an even greater diffusion of power within our military (in the Army and Marines) than most of us realize. Pragmatic behavior daily subverts antiquated structures, such as divisions and traditional staffs. We keep the old names, but the behaviors are changing. What, other than its flag, does the division of 1999 have in common with the division of World War II? Even as traditionalists resist the reformation of the force, the "anarchy" of lieutenants is shaping the Army of tomorrow. Battalion commanders do not understand what their lieutenants are up to, and generals would not be able to sleep at night if they knew what the battalion commanders know. While we argue about change, the Army is changing itself. The Marines are doing a brilliant job of reinventing themselves while retaining their essence, and their achievement should be a welcome challenge to the Army. The Air Force and Navy remain rigidly hierarchical.

Culture is fate. Countries, clans, military services, and individual soldiers are products of their respective cultures, and they are either empowered or imprisoned. The majority of the world's inhabitants are prisoners of their cultures, and they will rage against inadequacies they cannot admit, cannot bear, and cannot escape. The recent chest-thumping of some Asian leaders about the degeneracy, weakness, and vulnerability of American culture was reminiscent of the ranting of Japanese militarists on the eve of the Pacific war. I do not suggest that any of those Asian leaders intend to attack us, only that they are wrong. Liberty always looks like weakness to those who fear it.

In the wake of the Soviet collapse, some commentators declared that freedom had won and history was at an end. But freedom will always find enemies. The problem with freedom is that it's just too damned free for tyrants, whether they be dictators, racial or religious supremacists, or abusive husbands. Freedom challenges existing orders, exposes bigotry, opens opportunity, and demands personal responsibility. What could be more threatening to traditional cultures? The advent of this new information age has opened a fresh chapter in the human struggle for, and with, freedom. It will be a bloody chapter, with plenty of computer smashing and head bashing. The number-one priority of non-Western governments in the coming decades will be to find acceptable terms for the flow of information within their societies. They will uniformly err on the side of conservatism—informational corruption—and will cripple their competitiveness in doing so. Their failure is programmed.

The next century will indeed be American, but it will also be troubled. We will find ourselves in constant conflict, much of it violent. The U.S. Army is going to add a lot of battle streamers to its flag. We will wage information warfare, but we will fight with infantry. And we will always surprise those critics, domestic and foreign, who predict our decline.

Spotting the Losers: Seven Signs of Noncompetitive States

When you leave the classroom or office and go into the world, you see at first its richness and confusions, the variety and tumult. Then, if you keep moving and do not quit looking, commonalties begin to emerge. National success is eccentric. But national failure is programmed and predictable. Spotting the future losers among the world's states becomes so easy it loses its entertainment value.

In this world of multiple and simultaneous revolutions—in technology, information, social organization, biology, economics, and convenience—the rules of international competition have changed. There is a global marketplace and, increasingly, a global economy. Although there is no global culture yet, American popular culture is increasingly available and wickedly appealing—and there are no international competitors in the field, only struggling local systems. Where the United States does not make the rules of international play, it shapes them by its absence.

The invisible hand of the market has become an informal but uncompromising lawgiver. Globalization demands conformity to the practices of the global leaders, especially to those of the United States. If you do not conform—or innovate—you lose. If you try to quit the game, you lose even more profoundly. The rules of international competition, whether in the economic, cultural, or conventional military field, grow ever more homogeneous. No government can afford practices that retard development. Yet such practices are often so deeply embedded in tradition, custom, and belief that the state cannot jettison them. That which provides the greatest psychological comfort to members of foreign cultures is often that which renders them noncompetitive against America's explosive creativity—our self-reinforcing dynamism fostered by law, efficiency, openness, flexibility, market discipline, and social mobility.

Traditional indicators of noncompetitive performance still apply: corruption (the most seductive activity humans can consummate while clothed); the absence of sound, equitably enforced laws; civil strife; or government attempts to overmanage a national economy. As change has internationalized and accelerated, however, new predictive tools have emerged. They are as simple as they are fundamental, and they are rooted in culture. The greater the degree to which a state—or an entire civilization—succumbs to these "seven deadly sins" of collective behavior, the more likely that entity is to fail to progress or even to maintain its position in the struggle for a share of the world's wealth and power. Whether analyzing military capabilities, cultural viability, or economic potential, these seven factors offer a quick study of the likely performance of a state, region, or population group in the coming century. These are the key "failure factors":

- Restrictions on the free flow of information.
- The subjugation of women
- Inability to accept responsibility for individual or collective failure.
- The extended family or clan as the basic unit of social organization.
- Domination by a restrictive religion.
- A low valuation of education.
- Low prestige assigned to work.

Zero-Sum Knowledge

The wonderfully misunderstood Clausewitzian trinity, expressed crudely as state-people-military, is being replaced by a powerful new trinity: the relationship between the state, the people, and information. In the latter phases of the industrial age, the free flow of quality information had already become essential to the success of industries and military establishments. If the internationalizing media toppled the Soviet empire, it was because that empire's battle against information sharing had hollowed out its economy and lost the confidence of its people. When a sudden flood of information strikes a society or culture suffering from an information deficit, the result is swift destabilization. This is now a global phenomenon.

Today's "flat-worlders" are those who believe that information can be controlled. Historically, information always equaled power. Rulers and civilizations viewed knowledge as a commodity to be guarded, a thing finite in its dimensions and lost when shared. Religious institutions viewed knowledge as inflammatory and damnable, a thing to be handled carefully and to advantage, the nuclear energy of yesteryear. The parallel to the world public's view of wealth is almost exact—an instinctive conviction that information is a thing to be gotten and hoarded, and that its possession by a foreign actor means that it has been, by vague and devious means, robbed from oneself and one's kind. But just as wealth generates wealth, so knowledge begets knowledge. Without a dynamic and welcoming relationship with information as content and process, no society can compete in the postindustrial age.

Information-controlling governments and knowledge-denying religions cripple themselves and their subjects or adherents. If America's streets are not paved with gold, they are certainly littered with information. *The availability of free, high-quality information, and a people's ability to discriminate between high- and low-quality data, are essential to economic development beyond the manufacturing level.* Whether on our own soil or abroad, those segments of humanity that fear and reject knowledge of the world (and, often, of themselves) are condemned to failure, poverty, and bitterness.

The ability of most of America's workforce to cope psychologically and practically with today's flood of data, and to cull quality data from the torrent, is remarkable—a national and systemic triumph. Even Canada and Britain cannot match it. Much of Japan's present stasis is attributable to that nation's struggle to make the transition from final-stage industrial power to information-age society. The more regulated flow of information with which Japan has long been comfortable is an impediment to postmodernism. While the Japanese nation ultimately possesses the synthetic capability to overcome this difficulty, its structural dilemmas are more informational and psychological than tangible—although the tangible certainly matters—and decades of educational reform and social restructuring will be necessary before Japan returns for another world-championship match.

In China, the situation regarding the state's attempt to control information and the population's inability to manage it is immeasurably worse. Until China undergoes a genuine cultural revolution that alters permanently and deeply the relationship among state, citizen, and information, that country will bog down at the industrial level. Its sheer size guarantees continued growth, but there will be a flattening in the coming decades, and decisively, China will have great difficulty making the transition from smokestack growth to intellectual innovation and service wealth.

The great class struggle of the twenty-first century will be for access to data, and it will occur in totalitarian and religious-regime states.

China, along with the world's other defiant dictatorships, suffers under an oppressive class structure, built on and secured by an informational hierarchy. The great class struggle of the twenty-first century will be for access to data, and it will occur in totalitarian and religious-regime states. The Internet may prove to be the most revolutionary tool since the movable-type printing press. History laughs at us all—the one economic analyst who would understand immediately what is happening in the world today would be a resurrected German "content provider" named Marx.

For countries and cultures that not only restrict but actively reject information that contradicts governmental or cultural verities, even a fully industrialized society remains an unattainable dream. Information is more essential to economic progress than an assured flow of oil. In fact, unearned, "found" wealth is socially and economically cancerous, impeding the development of healthy, enduring socioeconomic structures and values. If you want to guarantee an underdeveloped country's continued inability to perform competitively, grant it rich natural resources. The sink-or-swim poverty of northwestern Europe and Japan may have been their greatest natural advantage during their developmental phases. As the Shah learned and Saudi Arabia is proving, you can buy only the products, not the productivity, of another civilization.

As the Shah learned and Saudi Arabia is proving, you can buy only the products, not the productivity, of another civilization.

States that censor information will fail to compete economically, culturally, and militarily in the long run. The longer the censorship endures, the longer the required recovery time. Even after the strictures have been lifted, information-deprived societies must play an almost hopeless game of catch-up. In Russia, it will take at least a generation of genuine informational freedom to facilitate an economic takeoff that is not founded hollowly upon resource extraction, middleman profits, and the looting of industrial ruins. Unique China will need even longer to make the next great leap forward from industrial to informational economy—we have at least half a century's advantage. Broad portions of the planet may never make it. We will not need a military to deal with foreign success, but to respond to foreign failure—which will be the greatest source of violence in coming decades.

If you are looking for an easy war, fight an information-controlling state. If you are looking for a difficult investment, invest in an information-controlling state. If you are hunting a difficult conflict, enter the civil strife that arises after the collapse of an information-controlling state. If you are looking for a good investment, find an emerging or "redeemed" state unafraid of science, hard numbers, and education.

A Woman's Place

Vying with informational abilities as a key factor in the reinvigoration of the U.S. economy has been the pervasive entry of American women into the educational process and the workplace. When the stock market soars, thank Elizabeth Cady Stanton and the suffragettes, not just their beneficiary, Alan Greenspan. After a century and a half of struggle by English and American women, the U.S. economy now operates at a wartime level of human-resource commitment on a routine basis.

Despite eternally gloomy headlines, our country probably has the lowest wastage rate of human talent in the world. The United States is so chronically hungry for talent that we drain it from the rest of the planet at a crippling pace, and we have accepted that we cannot squander the genius of half our population. Even in Europe, "overskilling," in which inherent and learned abilities wither in calcified workplaces, produces social peace at the cost of cultural and economic lethargy, security at the price of mediocrity. The occasional prime minister notwithstanding, it is far rarer to encounter a female executive, top professional, or general officer in that mythologized, "more equitable" Europe than in the United States. Life in America may not be fair, but neither is it stagnant. What we lose in security, we more than compensate for in opportunity.

While Europe sleepwalks toward a thirty-five-hour work-week, we are moving toward the thirty-five-hour day. The intense performance of our economy would be unattainable without the torrent of energy introduced by competitive female job candidates. American women revolutionized the workforce and the workplace. Future social and economic historians will probably judge that the entry of women into our workforce was the factor that broke the stranglehold of American trade unions and gave a new lease on life to those domestic industries able to adapt. American women were the Japanese cars of business-labor relations: better, cheaper, dependable, and they defied the rules. Everybody had to work harder and smarter to survive, but the results have been a spectacular recovery of economic leadership and soaring national wealth.

Change that men long resisted and feared in our own country resulted not only in greater competition for jobs but also in the creation of more jobs, and not in the rupture of the economy but in its assumption of imperial dimensions (in a quirk of fate, already privileged males are getting much richer, thanks to the effects of feminism's triumph on the stock market). Equality of opportunity is the most profitable game going, and American capitalism has realized the wisdom of becoming an evenhanded consumer of skills. Despite serious exclusions and malignant social problems, we are the most efficient society in history. When Europeans talk of the dignity of the working man, they increasingly mean the right of that man to sit at a desk doing nothing or to stand at an idling machine. There is a huge difference between just being employed and actually working.

The math isn't hard. Any country or culture that suppresses half its population, excluding them from economic contribution and wasting energy keeping them out of school and the workplace, is not going to perform competitively with us. The standard counterargument heard in failing states is that there are insufficient jobs for the male population, thus it is impossible to allow women to compete for the finite incomes available. The argument is archaic and wrong. When talent enters a workforce, it creates jobs. Competition improves performance. In order to begin to compete with the American leviathan and the stronger of the economies of Europe and the Far East, less-developed countries must maximize their human potential. Instead, many willfully halve it.

The point isn't really the fear that women will steal jobs in country X. Rather, it's a fundamental fear of women—or of a cultural caricature of women as incapable, stupid, and worrisomely sexual. If, when you get off the plane, you do not see men and women sitting together in the airport lounge, put your portfolio or treaty on the next flight home.

It is difficult for any human being to share power already possessed. Authority over their women is the only power many males will ever enjoy. From Greece to the Ganges, half the world is afraid of girls and gratified by their subjugation. It is a prescription for cultural mediocrity, economic failure, and inexpressible boredom. The value added by the training and utilization of our female capital is an American secret weapon.

Blaming Foreign Devils

The cult of victimhood, a plague on the least successful elements in our own society, retards the development of entire continents. When individuals or cultures cannot accept responsibility for their own failures, they will repeat the behaviors that led to failure. Accepting responsibility for failure is difficult, and correspondingly rare. The cultures of North America, Northern Europe, Japan, and Korea (each in its own way) share an unusual talent for looking in the mirror and keeping their eyes open. Certainly, there is no lack of national vanity, prejudice, subterfuge, or bad behavior.

But in the clutch we are surprisingly good at saying, "We did it, so let's fix it."

The cult of victimhood, a plague on the least successful elements in our own society, retards the development of entire continents.

In the rest of the world, a plumbing breakdown implicates the CIA and a faltering currency means that George Soros—the Hungarian-born American billionaire, fund manager, and philanthropist—has been sneaking around in the dark. Recent accusations of financial connivance made against Mr. Soros and then against the Jews collectively by Malaysia's Prime Minister Mahathir only demonstrated that Malaysia's ambitions had gotten ahead of its cultural capacity to support them. Even if foreign devils are to blame—and mostly they are not—whining and blustering does not help. It only makes you feel better for a little while, like drunkenness, and there are penalties the morning after.

The failure is greater where the avoidance of responsibility is greater. In the Middle East and Southwest Asia, oil money has masked cultural, social, technical, and structural failure for decades. The military failure of the regional states has been obvious, consistent, and undeniable, but the locals sense—even when they do not fully understand—their noncompetitive status in other spheres as well. It is hateful and disorienting to them. Only the twin blessings of Israel and the United States, on which Arabs and Persians can blame even their most egregious ineptitudes, enable a fly-specked pretense of cultural viability.

In contrast, Latin America has made tremendous progress. Not long ago, the gringos were to blame each time the lights blinked. But with the rise of a better-educated elite and local experience of economic success, the leadership of Latin America's key states has largely stopped playing the blame game. Smaller states and drug-distorted economies still chase scapegoats, but of the major players, only Mexico still indulges routinely in the transfer of all responsibility for its problems to Washington, D.C.

Family Values

After the exclusion of women from productive endeavors, the next worst wastage of human potential occurs in societies where the extended family, clan, or tribe is the basic social unit. Although family networks provide a safety net in troubled times, offering practical support and psychological protection, and may even build a house for you, they do not build the rule of law, democracy, legitimate corporations, or free markets. Where the family or clan prevails, you do not hire the best man (to say nothing of the best woman) for the job, you hire Cousin Luis. You do not vote for the best man, you vote for Uncle Ali. And you do not consider cease-fire deals or shareholder interests to be matters of serious obligation.

Such cultures tend to be peasant based or of peasant origin, with the attendant peasant's suspicion of the outsider and of authority. Oligarchies of landed families freeze the pattern in time. There is a preference for a dollar grabbed today over a thousand dollars accrued in the course of an extended business relationship. Blood-based societies operate under two sets of rules: one, generally honest, for the relative; and another, ruthless and amoral, for deals involving the outsider. The receipt of money now is more important than the building of a long-term relationship. Such societies fight well as tribes but terribly as nations.

At its most successful, this is the system of the Chinese diaspora, but that is a unique case. The Darwinian selection that led to the establishment and perpetuation of the great Chinese merchant families (and village networks), coupled with the steely power of southern China's culture, has made this example an exception to many rules. More typical examples of the *Vetternwirtschaft* system are Iranian businesses, Nigerian criminal organizations, Mexican political and drug cartels, and some American trade unions.

Where blood ties rule, you cannot trust the contract, let alone the handshake. Nor will you see the delegation of authority so necessary to compete in the modern military or economic spheres. Information and wealth are assessed from a zero-sum worldview. Corruption flourishes. Blood ties produce notable family successes, but they do not produce competitive societies.

That Old-Time Religion

Religion feeds a fundamental human appetite for meaning and security, and it can lead to powerful social unity and psychological assurance that trumps science. Untempered, it leads to xenophobia, backwardness, savagery, and economic failure. The more intense a religion is, the more powerful are its autarchic tendencies. But it is impossible to withdraw from today's world.

Limiting the discussion to the sphere of competitiveness, there appear to be two models of socioreligious integration that allow sufficient informational and social dynamism for successful performance. First, religious homogeneity can work if, as in the case of Japan, religion is sufficiently subdued and malleable to accommodate applied science. The other model—that of the United States—is of religious coexistence, opening the door for science as an "alternative religion." Americans have, in fact, such wonderful plasticity of mind that generally even the most vividly religious can disassociate antibiotic drugs from the study of Darwin and the use of birth-control pills from the strict codes of their churches. All religions breed some amount of schism between theology and social practice, but the American experience is a marvel of mental agility and human innovation.

The more dogmatic and exclusive the religion, the less it is able to deal with the information age, in which multiple "truths" may exist simultaneously, and in which all that cannot be proven empirically is inherently under assault. We live in a time of immense psychological dislocation—when man craves spiritual certainty even more than usual. Yet our age is also one in which the sheltering dogma cripples individuals and states alike. The price of competitiveness is the courage to be uncertain—not an absence of belief, but a synthetic capability that can at once accommodate belief and its contradictions. Again, the United States possesses more than its share of this capability, while other societies are encumbered by single dominant religions as hard, unbending, and ultimately brittle as iron. Religious toleration also means the toleration of scientific research, informational openness, and societal innovation. "One true path" societies and states are on a path that leads only downward.

For those squeamish about judging the religion of another, there is a shortcut that renders the same answer on competitiveness: examine the state's universities.

Learning Power and Earning Power

The quality of a state's universities obviously reflects local wealth, but even more important, the effectiveness of higher education in a society describes its attitudes toward knowledge, inquiry versus dogma, and the determination of social standing. In societies imprisoned by dogmatic religions, or in which a caste or class system predetermines social and economic outcomes, higher education (and secular education in general) often has low prestige and poor content. Conversely, in socially mobile, innovative societies, university degrees from quality schools appear indispensable to the ambitious, the status conscious, and the genuinely inquisitive alike.

There are many individual and some cultural exceptions, but they mostly prove the rule. Many Indians value a university education highly—not as social confirmation, but as a means of escaping a preassigned social position. The privileged of the Arabian Peninsula, on the other hand, regard an American university degree (even from a booby-prize institution) as an essential piece of jewelry, not unlike a Rolex watch. In all cultures, there are individuals hungry for self-improvement and, sometimes, for knowledge. But statistically, we can know a society, and judge its potential, by its commitment to education, with universities as the bellwether. Not all states can afford their own Stanford or Harvard, but within their restraints, their attempts to educate their populations still tell us a great deal about national priorities and potential. Commitment and content cannot fully substitute for a wealth of facilities, but they go a long way, whether we speak of individuals or of continents.

Any society that starves education is a loser. Cultures that do not see inherent value in education are losers. This is even true for some of our own subcultures—groups for whom education has little appeal as means or end—and it is true for parts of Latin America, sub-Saharan Africa, and the Arab world. A culture that cannot produce a single world-class university is not going to conquer the world in any sphere.

America's universities are triumphant. Once beyond the silly debates (or monologues) in the liberal arts faculties, our knowledge industry has no precedent or peer. Even Europe's most famous universities, on the Rhine or the Seine, are rotting and overcrowded. We attract the best faculty, the best researchers, and the best student minds from the entire world. This is not a trend subject to reversal; rather, it is self-reinforcing.

Yet there is even more to American success in education than four good years at the "College of Musical Knowledge." The United States is also far ahead of other states in the flexibility and utility of its educational system. Even in Europe, the student's fate is determined early—and woe to the late bloomer. You choose your course, or have it chosen for you, and you are more or less stuck with it for life. In Germany, long famous for its commitment to education, the individual who gains a basic degree in one subject and then jumps to another field for graduate work is marked as a *Versager,* a failure. In the U.S. system, there are second, third, and fourth chances. This flexible approach to building and rebuilding our human capital is a tremendous economic asset, and it is compounded by the trend toward continuing education in midlife and for seniors.

A geriatric revolution is occurring under our noses, with older Americans becoming "younger" in terms of capabilities, interests, and attitudes—and much more apt to continue contributing to the common good. In the early decades of the next century, many Americans may hit their peak earning years not in their fifties but in their sixties—then seventies. This not only provides sophisticated talent to the labor pool but also maintains the worker as an asset to, rather than a drain upon, our nation's economy. For all the fuss about the future of Social Security, we may see a profound attitudinal change in the next generation, when vigorous, high-earning seniors come to regard retirement as an admission of failure or weakness, or just a bore. At the same time, more twenty-year-old foreigners than ever will have no jobs at all.

Investments in our educational system are "three-fers": they are simultaneously investments in our economic, social, and military systems. Education is our first line of defense. The rest of the world can be divided into two kinds of societies, states, and cultures—those that struggle and sacrifice to educate their members, and those that do not. Guess who is going to do better in the hypercompetitive twenty-first century?

Workers of the World, Take a Nap!

Related to, but not quite identical with, national and cultural attitudes toward education is the attitude toward work. Now, everyone has bad days at the office, factory, training area, or virtual workplace, and the old line "It's not supposed to be fun—that's why they call it work," enjoys universal validity. Yet there are profoundly different attitudes toward work on this planet. While most human beings must work to survive, there are those who view work as a necessary evil and dream of its avoidance, and then there are societies in which people hit the lottery and go back to their jobs as telephone linemen. In many subsets of Latin American culture, for example, there are two reasons to work: first to survive, then to grow so wealthy that work is no longer necessary. It is a culture in which the possession of wealth is not conceptually related to a responsibility to work. It is the get-rich-quick, big-bucks-from-heaven dream of some of our own citizens. The goal is not achievement but possession, not accomplishment but the power of leisure.

Consider any culture's heroes. Generally, the more macho or male-centric the culture, the less emphasis there will be on steady work and achievement, whether craftsmanship or Nobel Prize-winning research, and the more emphasis there will be on wealth and power as the sole desirable end (apart, perhaps, from the occasional religious vocation). As national heroes, it's hard to beat Bill Gates. But even a sports star is better than a major narco-trafficker.

Generally, societies that do not find work in and of itself "pleasing to God and requisite to Man" tend to be highly corrupt (low-education and dogmatic-religion societies also are statistically prone to corruption, and if all three factors are in play, you may not want to invest in the local stock exchange or tie your foreign policy to successful democratization). The goal becomes the attainment of wealth by any means.

Workaholic cultures, such as that of North America north of the Rio Grande, Japan, South Korea, and some other East Asian states, can often compensate for deficits in other spheres, such as a lack of natural resources or a geographical disadvantage. If a man or woman has difficulty imagining a fulfilling life without work, he or she probably belongs to a successful culture. Work has to be seen as a personal and public responsibility, as good in and of itself, as spiritually necessary. Otherwise, the society becomes an "evader" society. Russia is strong, if flagging, on education. But the general attitude toward work undercuts education. When the characters in Chekhov's *Three Sisters* blather about the need to find redemption through work, the prescription is dead-on, but their lives and their society have gone so far off the rails that the effect is one of satire. States and cultures "win" just by getting up earlier and putting in eight honest hours and a little overtime.

If you are seeking a worthy ally or business opportunity, go to a midlevel government office in country X an hour before the local lunchtime. If everybody is busy with legitimate work, you've hit a winner. If there are many idle hands, get out.

Using This Knowledge to Our Advantage

Faced with the complex reality of geopolitics and markets, we must often go to country X, Y, or Z against our better judgment. Despite failing in all seven categories, country X may have a strategic location that makes it impossible to ignore. Country Y may have an internal market and regional importance so significant that it would be foolish not to engage it, despite the risks. Country Z may have resources that make a great deal of misery on our part worth the sufferance. Yet even in such situations, it helps to know what you are getting into. Some countries would devour investments as surely as they would soldiers. Others just demand savvy and caution on our part. Yet another might require a local ally or partner to whom we can make ourselves indispensable. Whether engaging militarily or doing business in another country, it gives us a tremendous advantage if we can identify four things: their image of us, their actual situation, their needs, and the needs they perceive themselves as having (the four *never* connect seamlessly).

There are parallel dangers for military men and businessmen in taking too narrow a view of the challenges posed by foreign states. An exclusive focus on either raw military power or potential markets tells us little about how people behave, believe, learn, work, fight, or buy. In fact, the parallels between military and business interventions grow ever greater, especially since these form two of the legs of our new national strategic triad, along with the export of our culture (diplomacy is a minor and shrinking factor, its contours defined ever more rigorously by economics).

The seven factors discussed above offer a pattern for an initial assessment of the future potential of states that interest us. Obviously, the more factors present in a given country, the worse off it will be—and these factors rarely appear in isolation. Normally, a society that oppresses women does so under the aegis of a restrictive dominant religion that also insists on the censorship of information. Societies lacking a strong work ethic rarely value education.

In the Middle East, it is possible to identify states where all seven negatives apply; in Africa, many countries score between four and seven. Countries that formerly suffered communist dictatorships vary enormously, from Poland and the Czech Republic, with only a few rough edges, to Turkmenistan, which scores six out of seven. Latin America has always been more various than *Norteamericanos* realized, from feudal Mexico to dynamic, disciplined Chile.

Ultimately, our businesses have it easier than our military in one crucial respect: business losses are counted in dollars, not lives. But the same cultural factors that will shape future state failure and spawn violent conflicts make it difficult to do business successfully and legally. We even suffer under similar "rules of engagement," whether those placed on the military that dictate when a soldier may shoot or the legal restraints under which U.S. businesses must operate, imposing a significant disadvantage vis-à-vis foreign competitors.

As a final note, the biggest pitfall in international interactions is usually mutual misunderstanding. We do not understand them, but they do not understand us either—although, thanks to the Americanization of world media, they imagine that they do. From megadeals that collapsed because of Russian rapacity to Saddam's conviction that the United States would not fight following his invasion of Kuwait, foreign counterparts, rivals, and opponents have whoppingly skewed perceptions of American behaviors. In the end, military operations and business partnerships are like dating—the advantage goes to the player who sees with the most clarity.

We are heading into a turbulent, often violent new century. It will be a time of great dangers and great opportunities. Some states will continue to triumph, others will shift their relative positions, many will fail. The future will never be fully predictable, but globalization means the imposition of uniform rules by the most powerful actors. They are fundamentally economic rules. For the first time, the world is converging toward a homogeneous system, if not toward homogeneous benefits from that system. The potential of states is more predictable within known parameters than ever before.

We have seen the future, and it looks like us.

Our New Old Enemies

Our enemies of the future will be enemies out of the past. As the U.S. armed forces put their faith and funding behind ever more sophisticated combat systems designed to remove human contact from warfare, mankind circles back to the misbehaviors of yesteryear. Technologies come and go, but the primitive endures. The last decade of this millennium has seen genocide, ethnic cleansing, the bloody rending of states, growing religious persecution, the ascendancy of international crime, an unprecedented distribution of weaponry, and the persistence of the warrior—the man of raw and selfish violence—as a human archetype. In the 1990s, our Gulf War was the sole conventional conflict of note. Both lopsided and inconclusive, it confirmed the new military paradigm: the United States is unbeatable on a traditional battlefield, but that battlefield is of declining relevance.

We have failed to ask the most basic military question: *who is our enemy?* Our ingrained response when asked such a question is to respond with the name of a country—ten years ago it was the Soviet Union, while today China is the answer preferred by lazy analysts and defense contractors anxious to sell the unnecessary to the uncritical. We are desperate for enemies who make sense to us, who certify our choices and grant us clarity of purpose. But the age of warfare between states is waning—it may return, but it is not the preeminent military challenge of the coming decades. We must ask that question, "Who is our enemy?" on a much deeper level. We must study the minds and souls of violent men, seeking to understand them on a level that our civilization has avoided for two thousand years. We can no longer blame atrocities and the will to violence on the devil, or on mistaken ideologies, or even on childhood deprivations. None of the cherished explanations suffice. In this age of technological miracles, our military needs to study mankind.

Morally, the best among us may be those who argue for disarmament. But they are mistaken. The heart of the problem is not the weapon, but the man who builds and wields it. Were we to eliminate all weapons of mass destruction, as well as every last handgun and pocketknife, the killers among us would take up wooden clubs or rocks. The will to violence is within us—it is not merely a function of the availability of tools.

Man, not space, is the last frontier. We must explore him.

It should not surprise us that religions have done a better job of locating man's desires and impulses than have secular analysts, whether Hegel, Freud, or media critics. Religions handle the raw clay, and only those that address all of man's potential shapes survive. We are defined by the full range of our desires and behaviors, not only by those worthy of emulation. Successful religions grasp our totality (and our fears). Whereas social orders are concerned with surface effects, religions look within. And every major religion has a prohibition against killing. There would be no need for such rules were man not a killer by nature.

In the Judeo-Christian heritage, there is a commandment that believers credit directly to the writing finger of God: "Thou shalt not kill." Think about that. Overall, the ten commandments did a remarkable job of cataloging human frailty. As behavioral rules they are as valid for today's techno-civilization as they were for the dreary near-Orient of three thousand years ago. Those prohibitions acknowledged the most destructive things that we humans are apt to do, and they warned us not to do them. The warning not to kill was the bluntest commandment.

For the moment, lay aside the concept of the Old Testament as a sacred book and consider it as a documentary of human behavior: it is drenched in violence, and its moral tenets arose in response to a violent world. It begins with the plight of two refugees—Adam and Eve—and moves swiftly to the fratricide of their children. In book after book, we encounter massacre, genocide, ethnic cleansing, rape, plunder, kidnapping, assassination, ineradicable hatreds, and endless warfare. The fall of civilizations is reported with a merciless eye, and cities vanish with a terse comment. It sounds like the twentieth century: humanity is consistent.

Historians, however, are inconsistent. Today, we have moved away from our earlier view of civilization as a process of constant improvement, with Western civilization as man's crowning achievement. Yet the most vociferous multiculturalists and antimodernists, who imagine virtue in all that is foreign, still insist thoughtlessly that humankind is perfectable, if only we would take the latest scholarship on the mating habits of aborigines more seriously. I do not believe that man has improved. There is no evidence for it. Are we better than Christ, the Buddha or Mohammed, than Socrates, Ulug Begh, Maimonides, or Saint Francis? Fashions, conveyances, medicines, communications, and the sophistication of governmental structures have all evolved. Man has not. Man is the constant. Saddam is Pharoah, and Cain will always be with us.

I have chosen religious texts and figures as examples because you know them and they resonate. Is there a more powerful, cautionary myth for a military man than that of Cain and Abel? Throughout both testaments, we encounter violent actors and soldiers. They face timeless moral dilemmas. Interestingly, their social validity is not questioned even in the Gospels. Although the New Testament is often ambivalent toward soldiers, the thrust of the texts is to improve rather than abolish the soldiery. It is assumed that soldiers are, however regrettably, *necessary*. In Luke, soldiers approach John the Baptist asking, "What shall we do?" John does not tell them to put aside their arms. Rather, he answers them, "Rob no one by violence or by false accusation, and be content with your wages." Would that the generals and admirals involved in procurement might heed that advice today.

The Bible does not sugarcoat man's nature. Belief is not required—read it as a document and you will get a better picture of the very human enemies our soldiers will face in the next century than any work of contemporary scholarship or speculation provides. From child warriors to fanatics who revel in slaughter, man's future is written in man's past.

Still, if you are uneasy with the Old Testament as a catalog of human behaviors, substitute another work, the *Iliad*. It is the fountainhead of our civilization's secular literature. That epic begins with an argument over raping rights, proceeds through slaughter and betrayal, and has genocide as its goal. It is about the wreckage of Yugoslavia.

In our staff and war colleges, we still read Thucydides—not for the history, but for the immediacy. Has there been another historian since the Greek twilight who matched his wonder at man's stubborn imperfection, at his ineradicable nature?

Literature is history with the truth left in. I believe that we can profit from the study of the classical texts as never before. The veneer of civilization—so recent and fragile—is being stripped from much of the world. The old problems are today's problems—and tomorrow's. If we want to know "Who is our enemy?" we must look within.

I believe that mankind is a constant in a changing world. We love the familiar, and find change hard. The conflicts in which our military will engage in the coming years will have many topical causes; at bottom, however, there will be only two: man's nature, and the impact of change upon him.

The Muezzin and the Microchip

Whether or not we as individuals believe in a divine being, we can recognize religion as the most supple and consistently effective behavior-modification tool available to mankind. Now if you study religions—and the soldier who does not know what his enemy believes fights blindly—you will find that virtually all of them have two myths in common: a creation myth, and the myth of a lost golden age. The need for a creation story to explain our origins is self-evident—it responds to the adult counterpart of the child who wants to know from whence his little sister came. But the myth of a lost golden age, of the white and shining temple before the fall, is directly relevant to understanding our enemies.

We live in an age of unprecedented change. This is statistical fact. Never before has so much happened on so many levels with such breathtaking speed. Developments in a wide range of disciplines tumble over one another in a practical and psychological avalanche. Whether we speak of social structures and gender relations, medicine, communications and the utility of information, the changing nature of work and wealth, convenience and the shape of the inhabited landscape, or the sheer revolution of choice available to our citizens, our society has undergone a greater degree of intense and layered change than has any human system in history. It is a tribute to the robustness of our civilization that we have coped so well with change thus far. Other civilizations and cultures (and some individuals everywhere) are less resilient and are not coping effectively; in fact, they are decaying. And the decay of a culture is the human equivalent of the decay of atomic particles.

We live in an age when even the most adept, confident man or woman feels the earth shifting underfoot. In the parlance of strategic theorists, change is destabilizing. In the experience of the human being enduring it, change is confusing, threatening, and often hurtful. In the great scheme of things, most change turns out to be positive for most people. But it is only rarely so perceived.

Especially as we grow older, our eyes play tricks on us—we are more likely to see that which is lost than that which is gained. How often do we hear our colleagues, friends, or relatives complain about the passing of the good old days or how much better things were under the old boss (forgetting how that boss was resented during his or her tenure)?

Experience is of two kinds: that which we undergo, and that which we remember. Those "good old days" were not better. If man has not developed much, his (and certainly her) opportunities have. But we long for the certainty of that which we have known, suffered, and survived—especially when it lies at a safe distance. When I was a kid, a drugstore in my hometown displayed a poster showing a little boy lowering a bucket into a well. The print read, "Remember how sweet the water was from the old well? It was the leading cause of typhoid fever." I have never encountered a more succinct description of man's relationship to change. In our memories, we sweeten the waters of the past and erase the dirt and the sickness from the myths we make of our experience.

Men fight for myths, not for truth.

Those myths of the lost golden age are most seductive in turbulent times. In the ferocity, confusion, and competition of the moment, we *need* to believe that things were not always so hard or so unfair, that there was a time of greater kindness and justice, when man's better qualities prevailed—and that such an epoch might return, if only we take the correct actions. Whether a radicalized mullah aching to turn back the clock to the days of the great caliphs, or a weekend militiaman in the Midwest longing for the surety of a misremembered childhood, the impulse to believe that times were better once upon a time is universal.

The experience of change and the consequent impulse to gild the past are timeless elements of the human saga. I wrote above that we live in an age of unprecedented change. This is true. Yet it is also true that men and women in past ages have lived through times of then-unprecedented change. They, too, have felt the earth shake beneath their feet and heard the heavens rumble. Accounts of the early days of the locomotive and telegraph are packed with wonder and warning. An early weapon of mass destruction, the crossbow, was outlawed in its time by secular authorities and by the pope. Poets have always wept over the prosaic nature of their own ages, when the beauty of the past lay murdered by the practical. Can we imagine the shock to the people of the ancient Middle East upon the arrival of bronze weapons? How the villager must have recoiled from the stench and temptation of the rising city. The first wooden cask would have excited mockery and the insistence by the old guard that wine was meant to ferment in clay pots, and that was that. The potato, the most revolutionary food in modern history, terrified Europeans when it was first imported, inspiring the belief that it caused leprosy, among other diseases. The information is lost to us now, but try to imagine the shock that the first laws codified by a state had on ancient populations governed until then by custom and by fear of the supernatural. For that matter, imagine the shock that a legitimate, enforced code of law would have on Russia or Mexico today.

With man's inherent fear of change, it is astonishing how intensely we have developed our civilizations, if not ourselves. We have changed the world— but all we have changed about ourselves are our table manners.

The longing for the preservation or resurrection of an old order, real or fantastic, is the key to understanding much of the world's disorder. Even when our enemies are not personally motivated by the fear of change, it is the fears of their neighbors that grant those enemies opportunity. Wrapping themselves in the cloak of this convenient cause, they exploit any rupture between the governing and the governed, any gulf between a prospering "progressive" elite and the stagnating ranks of believers or traditionalist masses. The men who guide their followers to massacre understand the power of a call to the banner of nationalism or an appeal to tribal supremacy or an invitation to do some god's cleansing work with fire and sword. Demagogues capitalize on the sense of a trust betrayed and the "evil" of the new. They are geniuses of blame. All their failures, and the failures of all their followers, will forever be the fault of someone else.

Men will fight to the death to cling to a just-bearable past rather than embrace a less certain future, no matter its potential.

In periods of great change, human beings respond by turning to religion and resuscitating tradition. In the age of science, the frightened turn to belief. Perhaps the truest of all our clichés is that "ignorance is bliss." Men and women do not want to know. They may be pleased to learn of the misfortunes of their neighbor—confessional television shows have their roots in tribal whispers—but they do not want to know that their way of life, of belief, of organizing, learning, producing, and fighting is a noncompetitive bust. The greatest impact of this information age is that it makes the global masses aware of their inadequacy.

The greatest impact of this information age is that it makes the global masses aware of their inadequacy.

At the height of the British Empire, the average imperial subject had no idea how his rulers lived. Today, the poor of the world's slums have awakened to the lifestyles of the rich and famous, courtesy of television, film, video, radio, cassettes, the self-justifications of kinsmen who have gone abroad and failed, and appalling local journalism. They do not, of course, grasp our reality. But they believe they do. The America they see is so rich and powerful it must be predatory. It *must* have robbed them to grow so rich. It has no right to be so rich. And it is unjust that they should not be so rich.

The media create instant myth. An illusion of America arrives, courtesy of lurid television serials, exaggerating Western wealth, ease, and sexuality. There is no mention of the sufferings of our ancestors on the long road to contemporary prosperity, or even of the workaday lives of average Americans today. It is as if our riches had fallen from the skies. It is an unbearable spectacle to those who have not.

At the same time, those who watch from abroad, appetites growing, find themselves less and less able to compete with the American juggernaut. Economic structures, the decline in the relative value of muscle power, educational inadequacies, social prohibitions and counterproductive customs, the ineffectiveness of civil law—these things and more constrict the potential of other cultures to compete with the West: the United States and our most culturally agile allies. Even cultures that appeared poised to break out to near equivalence with us, such as those of Southeast Asia, hit cultural ceilings—and such ceilings are made of iron, not glass.

Most analysis of the current plight of the Asian "tigers" focuses on economic issues, but the underlying problem is cultural: the human infrastructure could not support the level of success already achieved, let alone that which was desired. The most disappointing, and worrisome, aspect of the near collapse of Asian economies was not the financial losses but the alacrity with which the disappointed states, leaders, and people blamed foreigners for their misfortunes, when the problems were transparently homemade. Some also blamed their own minorities, especially the overseas Chinese. In Indonesia, we saw the return of ethnic pogroms. Even our South Korean allies responded to economic crisis with a tantrum of xenophobia. Hatred and revenge are always more satisfying than a sense of responsibility for one's own failure.

When nations and their underlying cultures fail to qualify in today's hypercompetitive world, they first complain. Then, if there is no turnaround, they kill. Iraq did not invade Kuwait in a burst of self-confidence, but from fear of economic decline and future inabilities. Tomorrow's enemies will be of two kinds—those who have seen their hopes disappointed, and those who have no hope. Do not worry about a successful China. Worry about a failing China.

And even a failing China is unlikely to become the threat defense charlatans would have us believe. China is culturally robust. Our most frequent opponents will rise from cultures on the rocks. In our grim century, Russia and Germany grew most dangerous after systems of cultural organization failed. Above all, this means that the Islamic world will be a problem for the foreseeable future, since it is unprepared to deal with the demands—and mandatory freedoms—of the postmodern age. Beyond that faded, failing civilization, watch out for other change-resistant cultures, from tribes and clans to states that never shook off feudal, agrarian mentalities (such as Mexico, or Russia and its determination to be a regional spoiler). None of these will threaten our homes; abroad, however, they will threaten our preferred order and the extraction of the wealth that pays for our homes.

Contrary to the myths of the old, pitiful Left, the United States did not build its new cultural-economic empire on the backs of the world's workers and peasants. But thanks to the information age, we will expand that empire at the expense of failing cultures, since the world insists on devouring our dross. The Left understood neither the time line nor the dynamics of history. And today's shriveled Left—hardly more than a campus entertainment—still gets one thing hugely wrong: the notion of an American determination to impoverish others. The United States prefers *prosperous* markets—starving masses don't buy much software (and they really do work on the Western conscience). But we cannot force people to be successful.

Those who fall by the wayside in global competition will have themselves, and their ancestors, to blame.

Sherman, Set the Way Back!

With the antimodern tide of fundamentalism that has swept away regimes and verities over the past two decades, we have come to accept, once again, that religious belief can turn violent. Yet, when we analyze our opponents, we insist on a hard, Joe Friday, "just the facts" approach that focuses on numbers, hardware, and perhaps a few of their leaders. We maintain a mental cordon sanitaire around military operations, ignoring the frightening impact of belief on our enemy's will and persistence. We accept the CNN reality of "mad mullahs" and intoxicated masses, yet we do not consider belief a noteworthy factor when assessing our combat opponents. Yet only plagues and the worst personal catastrophes excite the religious impulse in man to the extent that war does.

The interplay of religion and military violence deserves books, not just a few paragraphs. But begin with that which we know. In vague outline, we are all familiar with the Great Indian Mutiny, when the British East India Company's native levies, both Muslim and Hindu, reacted to a rumor that their new cartridges had been soiled with pig fat or beef lard by rising up and slaughtering their overlords. While any Marxist will tell you that there were structural factors at play in the Sepoy Mutiny and that the cartridges were but a catalyst, the fact remains that the most savage experience of the Victorian era was the butchery of the Mutiny—first the atrocities committed against British men, women, and children, then the slaughter perpetrated against the native population by the British, which was crueler still.

The Indian Mutiny offers only a hint at the religious violence once extant in the British Empire. London's imperial history offers an interesting study for today's problems; the overwhelming impact of industry-backed regiments against native masses, the shattering of established orders, the spiritual dislocations of the defeated—all this is replaying around us and will play on into the next century at fast-forward speed. Notably, Britain's most embarrassing defeats of the nineteenth century were dealt the empire not by other organized militaries but by true believers—whether the ferocious holy warriors of Afghanistan or the devout Calvinist Boers. Again and again, resistance to British influence or rule rallied around a religious identity, whether following the Mahdi in the Sudan or, in our own century, struggling to recreate Israel or a united, independent Ireland. Our own national introduction to imperial combat involved a Chinese revivalist order, the "Fists of Righteousness," or Boxers, and in the Philippines, the impassioned Muslim Moros proved a far tougher enemy for us than the conventional Spanish military.

And what of the impact of belief *within* armies? It is a war-movie truism that the frightened and dying turn to the chaplain, but if we argue individual cases, we might conclude that this is evidence of desperation, not of a genuine propulsion toward belief. Yet consider our own bloodiest conflict—the Civil War. It saw a widespread religious revival in blue ranks and gray—although as the South's condition worsened, the intensity of religious fervor in the Confederate armies grew extreme. Although it is unfashionable to say so, there is ample evidence that, for many on both sides, this was a holy war. Certainly, the hungry, ill-clothed men in the Army of Northern Virginia fought with the determination of martyrs. Stonewall Jackson *entered* the war a religious extremist and fought with a holy warrior's dedication. Sherman was a secular fanatic produced by an age of belief. His march from Atlanta to the sea, then northward through the Carolinas, was a crusade executed with a religious fervor, if without religious rhetoric. When we examine contemporary letters and reports, it is clear that God was very much with both sides.

This is an ancient phenomenon. Return to the *Iliad*. Read differently and more closely this time. Don't skim the long passages detailing sacrifices or the name-dropper poetry about squabbling gods. Look at what Homer tells us about belief in the ranks. The book begins with Agamemnon's defiance of the ordained order of things—a middle finger thrust up not only at Achilles but also at the gods. The Greek forces suffer for it. Plague sweeps them. The Trojans briefly turn the tide. *And the Greeks respond in terms of their religion*. The first step is not a new battlefield strategy, it is a religious revival. Even the king must be called to order. Penitence is in. Sacrifices must involve real sacrifice. Certainly, the return of Achilles to the fight boosts morale, but the Greeks also experience a renewed sense that the gods are on their side. Meanwhile, in threatened Troy, an otherworldly fatalism takes hold, dark prophecies ring out, and

Priam and his people search for an explanation of their impending fall in the will of the gods.

Of course, we do not read the *Iliad* that way. It is not our habit; we shy away from manifestations of faith, suspecting or ignoring them or, at best, analyzing them in the dehydrated language of the sociologist. But if we want to understand the warriors of the world, and the fury that drives them, we had better open our minds to the power of belief.

In our own Western cultural history, the fiercest military brutalities and the most savage wars were fought over faith, whether Crusades or defensive wars against Muslims, campaigns of suppression against dissenting Christians, the great religious wars of the sixteenth and especially seventeenth centuries, or the twentieth century's world wars between secular religions.

Now our history is playing out in other flesh. When Indonesian rioters murder Chinese merchants, or when the Sudanese Muslims who hold power butcher and enslave the Christians in their country's south, their behavior is not inhuman. On the contrary, it is timelessly human.

Beware of any enemy motivated by supernatural convictions or great moral schemes. Even when he is less skilled and ill equipped, his fervor may simply wear you down. Our military posture could not be more skewed. We build billion-dollar bombers, but we cannot cope with bare-handed belief.

The Shaman and the Gangster

If the intoxicated believer is one very dangerous extreme in the range of our enemies, the other is the man utterly free of belief or fear of the law or civilizing custom. When you encounter them together—the saint and the cynic in league— you have the most dangerous combination on earth. True believers and opportunists are a dynamic match, as many a successful televangelist instructs us. You see it in a sloppy fashion with Saddam and his belated attention to Islam, but also in the alliance between the current set of Kremlin bandits and the Orthodox Church.

From Algeria's religious terrorists to politicians anywhere who align themselves with religious movements whose convictions they privately do not share, it is often difficult for us to determine where the prophet ends and the profiteer begins, how much is about faith and how much about grabbing power. In such cases, we tend to err on the side of cynicism, preferring to impute base motives to our enemies (even as we imagine that those enemies are somehow redeemable). But slighting either side of the equation, the human potential for cynicism or for belief, brings us only half answers. In conflict, the saint and the cynic can complete each other without consciously understanding why their alliance works so well. Together, they combine the qualities of the cobra and the chameleon.

The most difficult thing for Americans in (and out of) uniform to face may be that even the most powerful military can, at most, briefly alter outward behaviors. We subdue belief only by killing the believer. From Somalia to Bosnia, the opportunist will bow to the threat of lethal power—until you turn your back. But no display of might will change the essence of either the man driven by God or the man driven by greed.

We have entered another age when empires begin to learn their limits. Although America has—and will maintain—informational dominance, we cannot dictate which information will be accepted and acted upon by foreign populations. We can flood them with our culture, shock them into doubt, sell them our wares—but we cannot make them behave as we would like, unless we are willing to commit brutalities on a scale that would destroy our own myth of ourselves.

Certainly, if sufficiently provoked, we are capable of killing plentifully and with enthusiasm. But such events are exceptional. In their balance and wisdom, the American people will fight genuine enemies, but they would not countenance the unprovoked slaughter of foreign populations over distant misbehaviors. The mark of our civilization's greatness is a simple but rare one: at this point in our social development, we would rather do good than evil, so long as it doesn't cost too much. It is a surprisingly rare quality.

In other regions of the globe, there is less interest in the inviolability of the individual. We face enemies whose sole motivation to refrain from killing is the fear of being killed. Nothing else moves them. It is difficult for Americans, with our lack of historical knowledge and our fuzzy notion of the validity of all cultures, to grasp the richness of hatred in this world. For all of our alarm over crime, most Americans live in an astonishingly safe environment. We are not threatened, and we behave cooperatively and corporately. But our safety is both the result of and contributor to our insularity. We lead sheltered lives. And we imagine that the rest of the world is just like us, only less privileged.

Hatred

The rest of the world is not like us. For all of our lingering prejudices, we have done a remarkable job of subduing our hatreds. Perhaps it is only the effect of wealth bounded by law that makes us such a powerful exception to history, but our lack of domestic faction is a miracle nonetheless. We are indescribably fortunate—but our good fortune has lulled us into our primary military and diplomatic weakness: we do not understand the delicious appeal of hatred.

We cannot understand how Serbs, Croats, and Bosnian Muslims could do that to each other. We cannot understand how Hutus and Tutsis could do that to each other. We do not understand how the Chinese could do that to the Tibetans. We do not understand how the Armenians and Azeris could do that to each other. We do not understand how the tribes of Sierra Leone or Liberia could do that to each other. We do not understand how India's Hindus and Muslims could do that to each other. We do not understand how the Russians and Chechens could do that to each other. We do not understand how Haitians, Somalis, Colombians, Mexicans, Indonesians, Sri Lankans, Congolese, Burundians, or the Irish could do that to each other.

Over the years, I have written about "warriors," the nonsoldiers, from guerrillas to narco-traffickers, whom we encounter and fight. In the past, I stressed the importance of recognizing five types of warriors: the scum of the earth, the average Joe who is drawn into the conflict as it drags on, demobilized military men, opportunists, and true believers. Now I worry about only two of these sources of conflict—the opportunists and the believers, the gangsters and the godly, the men unrestrained by morals and those whose iron morality is implacable. They are the centers of gravity. The others are swept along by the tide.

Man, the Killer

Of all the notions I have advanced over the years, the only one that has met with consistent rejection is the statement that men like to kill. I do not believe that all men like to kill. At the extreme, there are those saintly beings who would sacrifice their own lives before taking the life of another. The average man will kill if compelled to, in uniform in a war or in self-defense, but has no evident taste for it. Men react differently to the experience of killing. Some are traumatized. Others simply move on with their lives. But there is at least a minority of human beings—mostly male—who enjoy killing. That minority may be small, but it does not take many enthusiastic killers to trigger the destruction of a fragile society. Revolutions, pogroms, genocides, and civil wars are made not by majorities, but by minorities with the acquiescence of the majority. The majority may gloat or loot, but the killing minority drives history.

> *There is at least a minority of human beings — mostly male—who enjoy killing. That minority may be small, but it does not take many enthusiastic killers to trigger the destruction of a fragile society.*

Violence is addictive. Police know this. That's where the phrase "the usual suspects" comes from. In our society, the overwhelming majority of violent acts are committed by repeat offenders. Statistics would make us a violent nation; in fact, we are a peaceable people until aroused. The numbers are skewed because we have failed to deter recidivists.

Spouse and child abusers do not do it once—they repeat. Sex offenders—and sex crimes are all crimes of violence—are notorious repeat offenders. Most barroom brawls are begun by the same old troublemakers. Even in combat, when mortal violence is legal, most enemy combatants killed in close fighting appear to be killed by a small number of "high performers" in our ranks. Throughout history, many a combat hero has had difficulty adjusting to peace.

We reject the evidence of the human enthusiasm for violence because it troubles us and undercuts the image we have created of perfectible man. But violence has an undeniable appeal. Certainly, for the otherwise disenfranchised, it is the only response left. Perhaps the psychologists are right that much violence is a cry for help. But what both of those arguments really say is that violence, however motivated, is gratifying and empowering.

Religions and civilizations may be seen as attempts to discipline mankind, to trim our worst excesses. Traditionally, religions and civilizations acknowledged mankind's propensity for violence and imposed appropriate strictures. Certainly, no religion or civilization has believed that it could ignore violent behavior as peripheral. Yet our contemporary American approach is to treat violence as an aberration, the product of a terrible misunderstanding. It is the mentality of the born victim, of the spouse who believes every weeping apology, of the social worker who believes in the mass murderer's rehabilitation. Our willful denial of the full spectrum of man's nature, from the sublime to the beastly, is a privilege of our wealth. It is not a privilege that will be extended to our soldiers.

Look at the wreckage of this decade. Can we pretend that the massacre of half a million Rwandan Tutsis by their neighbors was carried out as a laborious chore? On the contrary, reports from the scene describe murderers intoxicated by their deeds. When we consider the ingenious cruelties perpetrated daily in Algeria, can we believe that the killers are forced to commit those atrocities against their inclinations? Will we pretend that the dead of Srebrenica were the victims of reluctant hands?

A meaningful sense of humanity demands that we ask hard questions about the nature of man. Military effectiveness in the coming decades will make the same demands. It will be terribly difficult for us. Our noble, unique elevation of the individual's worth is ill suited to a world in which our opponents regard the masses who follow them as surplus capital.

The American Myth of Peace

A corollary to the universal myth of a lost golden age is the recurring myth of the peaceable kingdom, where the lion lies down with the lamb and the spear is broken in two. This has long been a powerful myth in the American grain, carried from Europe in the first ships that sailed for New England. In those northern colonies, many of the early settlers belonged to dissident Protestant sects out to replicate the kingdom of God on earth. Many were pacifists or had strong pacifistic inclinations. They had been oppressed, and, no matter that they would become oppressors in their time, their experiences had condensed their vision of a just, ideal world to a diamond hardness.

Our founding parents fled Europe's dynastic struggles convinced that such wars, and by extension all wars, were ungodly. Later, they fought the Indians, then the French, then the British, then their hemispheric neighbors, then much of the world. But they never accepted war as being in the order of things. War was a terrible, unnatural misfortune, perpetrated by despots and madmen or spawned by injustice. But it was not a core human endeavor.

From that heritage we Americans have developed our ahistorical belief that all men want peace, that all conflict can be resolved through compromise and understanding. It leads to the diplomatic equivalent of Sunday night snake handling—faith in the power of negotiations to allay hatred. Because we are privileged and reasonably content with our corner of the planet, we find peace desirable. There is nothing wrong with this. The problem arises when we assume that all other men, no matter how discontented, jealous, disenfranchised, and insulted, want peace as well. Our faith in man is, truly, a blind faith.

Many human beings have no stake in peace. They draw no advantage from the status quo. We see this even in our own fortunate country. A disproportionate share of crime is committed by those with the least stake in society—the excluded and marginalized with little or nothing to lose. In this age of accelerating change, we, too, suffer from extreme fundamentalism concentrated at the lower end of the social spectrum (though not at the bottom among the drug-wrecked *Lumpenproletariat).* Consider the crimes that trouble us most. Gang crime occurs between those with the least to gain or lose from the social order the rest of us cherish. The Oklahoma City bombing was the work of a man who felt rejected by the society around him, who felt *wronged.* The repeated bombings of planned parenthood clinics consistently prove to be the work of low-skilled males who have turned to aggressive religious beliefs in which tolerance is intolerable. Dangerous true believers and violent opportunists are very much with us even in our own homeland.

We are, however, well positioned to moderate their excesses. Neither right-wing militias nor extreme fundamentalists are going to take over our country in the foreseeable future. But much of the world is less fortunate. Where there is less opportunity (sometimes none) and the existing, comforting order shrivels, human beings want validation and revenge. They cannot accept that their accustomed way of life is failing and that they are failing individually because of the behaviors to which their culture has conditioned them. They want someone to blame, and then they want revenge on that someone. A leader, secular or religious, has only to preach the gospel of foreign devils and dark conspiracies—to absolve his listeners of responsibility for their own failures—and he will find a willing audience.

Humans do not want change. They want their customs validated. They want more material possessions, but they do not want to alter their accustomed patterns of behavior to get those things. This is as true in America's inner cities as it is in the slums of Karachi or Cairo.

Humans do not want change. They want their customs validated. They want more material possessions, but they do not want to alter their accustomed patterns of behavior to get those things. This is as true in America's inner cities as it is in the slums of Karachi or Cairo.

Again, many human beings thrive on disorder. When the civil war ends, the party is over. Many of the difficulties in Bosnia today stem from warriors who built thriving black market and criminal networks during the fighting and do not want to let go of them. Often, those who do the bulk of the fighting are men ill equipped to prosper in peace. The gun is their professional tool. When they grow convinced by, or are at least cloaked in, nationalist or fundamentalist religious beliefs, they are vulnerable only to greater force. In Russia, much of the citizenry longs for the rule of law—even the harsh law of the past. But those who have enriched themselves during Russia's new "time of troubles" like the system just the way it is. Although our Department of State does not believe it, it is difficult to convince a prospering gangster that democracy and the rule of law will work to his advantage. Around the world, from Uganda to Abkhazia, it is difficult to persuade those whose only successes in life have come from the gun in their hand that they should hand over that gun. Being a warlord, or just the warlord's retainer, is a far more attractive prospect than digging a ditch for a living or, worse, failing to find work as a ditchdigger.

We profit from peace. Our opponents profit from conflict. It is as fundamental a mismatch as the one between our forces and theirs. When they try to play by our rules, whether in the military or economic sphere, we demolish them. When, however, we are forced to play by their rules, especially during military interventions, the playing field is not only leveled—it often tilts in their favor.

When we drive the warriors into a corner or defeat them, they will agree to anything. When our attention is elsewhere, they will break the agreement. Their behavior, natural to them, is unthinkable to us. And then they massacre.

We pride ourselves on our rationality, while avoiding reality. If we are to function effectively as diplomats and soldiers, we need to turn a dispassionate eye on mankind. We need to study the behavior of the individual and the mass, and to do it without stricture. We cherish the fiction that technology will be the answer to all our dilemmas. But our enemies know that flesh and blood form the irresistible answer to our technologies.

Troy and Jerusalem
Another cliché with a core of truth is that Americans are the new Romans, proprietors of a (near) universal empire based

on engineering and codification. Certainly, we guard the walls of our civilization against new barbarians. But the mundane parallels are more intriguing. First, even when the Romans behaved cruelly at the height of empire, it was a measured policy. Second, their military was tiny in proportion to the range of their empire, and their legions, while rarely defeated, were often astonished by the savagery of their opponents. Third, the Romans so cherished their civilized image of themselves that it blinded them to barbarian strengths.

Fanatics brought Rome down. We associate the fall of Rome with Alaric and the Visigoths and a jumble of other warrior peoples who swept in from the north for long weekends (as German tourists do today). But Rome's decline was slow, and the empire rotted from within. Romans loved the law— even under the worst emperors, the rule of law never disappeared entirely—and they grew convinced that peace was the natural order of things. Their judges sought equity and order, and their legalisms crippled them.

Let us return to our beginning and consider the New Testament. We are made in the image of Pilate the Roman. On his fateful day, he was annoyed, briefly, by a minor case he just wanted to put behind him. He did not understand the matter and did not even believe that it lay within his purview. He was baffled and annoyed by the local squabbles, failing to appreciate the social and religious complexities involved—and the greater implications. Jesus was beneath the consideration of Rome's threat analysts. Pilate just wanted the problem to go away. Capable of insight, cruelty, and greatness on other occasions, on the most important day of his life, the Roman was caught drowsing. He was the classic representative of empire, the patron saint of diplomats.

We can almost smell the heat of the day and taste the dust. Imagine Pilate's impatience with his translator and his disbelief that the shabby, battered figure before him could be the cause of such a fuss. There simply was not enough of a challenge in evidence to excite a Roman governor and gentleman of great affairs. When a perfunctory attempt at arbitration between the locals failed, Pilate "washed his hands" of the prisoner's fate, anxious to move on to serious business, or maybe just to lunch. He did let his soldiers do a bad day's work, but only because the Romans kept a careful monopoly on capital punishments.

Pilate was a symbol of weakening Rome and growing Roman self-doubt. He served at Rome's apogee, yet the cancer was already there. His descendants, preferring debate to decision, would be no match for the fanatics who could kill the sober and the just without blinking. Pilate stuck to the letter of the law, and the law damned him.

As empires fall—and I am not suggesting that our own empire will fall anytime soon—the people of the empire return to religion, to cults, to blood ties. Christianity, a liberating mystery religion of the suffering classes, had to struggle during the heyday of empire. But when the decline became impossible to deny, the new religion, with its revolutionary rhetoric, prospered. In prospering, it further accelerated the decline of the old order. The repressions were too little too late, and they were a counterproductive tool to wield against the followers of that particular creed. Rome turned scolds into martyrs. The Roman threat analysts had failed again.

The Romans were chronically late to respond to challenges in the age of the lesser Caesars. They loved stasis and remembrance. The destruction of Solomon's Temple in Jerusalem and the suppression of the Jewish kingdom were not signs of remaining imperial strength but signs of weakness, frustration, and decline. In its confident years, the Roman Empire had been absorptive and tolerant. For centuries, these qualities lent strength and co-opted new subjects—but ultimately, core identities and commitments to the Roman idea became fatally diffuse and diluted. It was those who refused to be absorbed and who rejected toleration, from the brute German tribes to the true believers from the eastern provinces, who outlasted the greatest empire the earth knew until our own century.

Rome's greatest failure was its inability to understand the changing world.

We can measure historical climates by reading the growth bands of a tree stump. We can measure the climate of a culture by noting its religious revivals or the advent of a new religion— each marks a time of great stress on the society. In 1999, we are living in the most passionately religious age in centuries. The future looks ferocious.

Leaving aside the threat from weapons of mass destruction, however, the United States appears invulnerable for the foreseeable future. Terrorists might annoy us, but we will triumph. We will, ultimately, find the strength of will to do what must be done. The problems raised in this essay affect the average, prosperous American citizen little, if at all. But it is the soldiers of our new empire, the men and women who serve in our expeditionary forces and deploy to subdue enemies we neglect to understand, who will pay the cost of our ignorance. They will still win, when allowed to do so. But more of them will suffer and die for lowered returns because of our unwillingness to face the complexity of mankind.

Come back now to Troy. Read that great poem one more time, without the prejudices we have learned. You will find that the triumphant Greeks were the devious, the barbarous, the murderous. The Trojans were the urban, civilized, and tolerant. Troy stood for learning, piety, and decency. Its mistake was to humiliate implacable barbarians, without the will to destroy them. The Trojans fought to be left alone in their comfortable world. The Greeks fought for revenge, spoils, and the pleasure of slaughter. The Greeks won. Ulysses, who finally inveigled a way through the city gates, was the first great Balkan warlord. Murdered King Priam was a decent man who watched the war from behind his walls and had to beg for the return of his son's mangled body. He was presidential in his dignity.

We are not Trojans. We are far mightier. We rule the skies and seas and possess the power to rule the land when we are sufficiently aroused. But we have not learned to understand, much less rule, minds and hearts and souls. The only moral we need to cull from the *Iliad* is that it is foolish to underestimate the complexity and determination of the killers from the other shore.

Fighting for the Future

If the United States musters the will, we will dominate the world in the twenty-first century and dictate the global security environment. Our dominion would be without precedent in extent, power, and decency. I believe that we could block wars between states, reduce the threat of weapons of mass destruction, interdict terrorists, destroy international criminal networks, and ultimately, transform the minds of violent actors and potential enemies.

The future holds great danger, but that danger will diminish to the extent that we pioneer new means of peace enforcement—and find the courage to use those means. If we are willing, we can secure a peaceful future that, although it will not eliminate evil from men's souls, will deliver a reduction in war, conflict, and violence that breaks with mankind's grim and sordid past. *We* can soothe this tormented earth. We need only the determination to exercise our strength, and the courage to believe that we are right.

There are two obstacles to a genuine Pax Americana in the coming century. The first is a series of technological barriers. We shall overcome these. The second—and far more challenging—is moral relativism. We must leave behind this era of self-debasement. American civilization is the most humane, hopeful, decent, magnetic, and generous of opportunity in history. It marks a break with all that has come before, leaving behind even northwestern Europe, with its drab cubicles of the spirit and pared-down lives. While we must study our excesses and failures, striving to correct or ameliorate them, it is time to focus again on that which is good, successful, and true in the American synthesis of cultures.

If we are willing, we can secure a peaceful future that, although it will not eliminate evil from men's souls, will deliver a reduction in war, conflict, and violence that breaks with mankind's grim and sordid past.

Without the United States, the twentieth century would have experienced the triumph of evil. With America, the twenty-first century might see the triumph of good. But we must accept the responsibilities of our power and our civilizing mission. We will be in a position to bring the world lasting peace. But to do so, we must say good-bye to the crippling notions that all cultures, no matter how odious, enjoy equivalent validity, and that even the most wicked foreign leader is inviolable in his person. The American peace will have to be on American terms, and those terms cannot be negotiable.

Ending Wars Between Military Systems

For the next few decades, warfare will continue to evolve. Despite growing asymmetries and disparities, it will remain recognizable to students of history. Wars between states and military systems will occur with less frequency but may prove surprisingly eruptive and large in scale. We do not know.

Yet, if we begin now, we can annihilate the tradition of conventional war by the middle decades of the twenty-first century—if not sooner. We have already begun the process with the deployment of intelligence systems of ever greater scope, definition, and penetrating power. Although imperfect, our targeting capability is without precedent, and it will continue to improve. We will be able to locate aggressors, except for the lonely gunmen in the urban depths. The next step will be to develop and field the systems necessary to destroy aggressors and killers within minutes of our decision to do so.

Although many of the current models and experiments sponsored by the U.S. armed forces are designed to justify the present way of doing business, some efforts, such as the Army After Next program, have begun to intuit the future—despite factional prejudice and a recent wave of poorly chosen leaders. The physical key to the next military revolution will be attack systems permanently deployed in near space that can, on order, destroy the vehicles, aircraft, missiles, and ships of any aggressor anywhere on the planet the moment a hostile actor violates or even threatens the territory of another state or entity—or uses military means to disrupt the internal rule of law in his own state. A combination of (all unmanned) geosynchronous, near-space picket systems with redeployable "fleet" systems, exploiting evolved physical principles and miniaturization, would patrol the surface of the earth and the atmosphere above it. The United States, embarked now upon a revolution of technological and informational wealth creation, will be able to afford such systems—if we learn to use the market, anti-corruption initiatives, and vigorous prosecutions to discipline the contractors with whom we do business.

In essence, we need to move beyond the vestiges of the Strategic Defense Initiative to a Strategic Enforcement Initiative, to graduate from a (much needed) defense of our homeland to a position of global dominance that precludes attacks on us and preempts local aggression. With our eyes on the distant future, we need to transform twentieth-century concepts, such as shooting down incoming missiles, into a regime so swift it destroys hostile missiles before they clear their silos or launchers.

The goal, initially, is not to interfere in the affairs of foreign states, as long as they behave humanely toward their populations. The first—realizable—step is to force an end to interstate warfare. We alone will have the wealth and power to do it—plus, we could collect defense taxes from states that benefit from our actions. As the world's only extant empire of law and justice, we also have the right and responsibility to do it. We need have no moral reservations about outlawing aggression and then enforcing that prohibition.

Destroying hostile warmaking systems will be the easiest part. Whether we eventually choose laser, particle, hypervelocity or yet-to-be-imagined attack systems, it is easy to visualize a U.S. Peace Force watching and waiting above the skies, prepared to open fire the moment an armored vehicle from an aggressor state enters a universally defined demilitarized buffer imposed on all states. Further, we must make it clear that aggressive actions mean that we would destroy not only the transgressing military systems but every other military means available to the aggressor country or nonstate entity. The least hostile military action would bring down a rain of fire from the heavens, destroying an attacker's military inventory, whether he has deployed it, hidden it, or simply left it behind in garrison. This could be the world's first disarmament program that works.

Should we have the moral authenticity to grasp this opportunity, we may at last see the withering away of military establishments, since they will prove unusable. Only constabularies and police forces need remain, except for our own forces and those of a few morally coincident allies, such as the other English-speaking, law-cherishing states. It will be in our power to eliminate one of the greatest scourges of human history. We will be damned if we fail to act.

The Goldfinger Paradigm

Before proceeding further, consider the limitations of mass imagination. Perhaps the greatest stumbling block for revolutionaries has been that the human collective is not programmed to envision a lavishly different future; rather, we fear any future that is not largely the same as the reality we know and have mastered. Human beings crave certainty, and that craving guarantees the success of dogmatic religions and fast-food restaurants. How long would McDonald's survive if its menu changed every day? What religion would thrive on a constantly fluctuating view of the hereafter?

We human beings want to know what we're getting. Far from adventurously pursuing the future, the masses avoid thinking about it except in the most platitudinous, neutered terms. Films set in the future, such as the *Star Wars* trilogy, succeed not because they celebrate change but because they assure us that, beyond the entertaining surface effects, the patterns of human experience and behavior remain indestructible. *Star Wars* imagined the future in the resonant terms of America's frontier myths, translating comforting clichés from the Wild West to the Wild Galaxies. "Futurist" films reassure us with their sameness to that which we know—the hero and heroine always reflect our contemporary values.

Individuals are more apt to imagine an evolved future than is the collective, but even those individuals usually occupy themselves with dreaming of improvements in their own lives—the reformed husband, the contented wife, the upright son and daughter, or simply an upturn in personal finances. Our daydreams of tomorrow occur in today's moral and physical context. We cannot even imagine the next decade's fashions, let alone its breakthrough technologies.

The film *Goldfinger* reached the theaters as I lurched through junior high school. It dazzled us with the "high-tech" gimmicks it imagined. View it again. Barely a generation old, it is watchable now only as a nostalgia piece. Although it does not spray oil slicks or machine-gun bullets, my midprice sedan incorporates far more technologies than the screenwriters—straining their imaginations—concocted for James Bond's Aston Martin. There is a deadly laser in the film that would not pass muster in a serious workshop today, to say nothing of a North American hospital. The film revolves around a demented magnate's hunger for gold—yet what is the relevance of gold today? There is no inkling of digital banking, of the instantaneous global shift of billions of dollars, of the remarkable commercialization of communications and knowledge, of the prosaic might of brokers and currency traders. The film was prescient in imagining the terrorist use of weapons of mass destruction, but its creators could not even design competitive golf clubs for its hero.

In its day, *Goldfinger* struck us all as stunningly high-tech in its vision. There were no personal computers on the screen, no satellite communications, no videos or microwave ovens, not even a fax machine (all these technologies—save the already existing satcoms—were but a decade or so in the future). Yet we were dazzled. The point is that, especially in this age of ever-accelerating technological developments, we cannot begin to imagine the full range of tools the future will bring us. When we do risk describing possible futures, they appear laughable and far-fetched to our contemporaries. Today is forever our paradigm and our intellectual prison. If your home was built ten years ago—no matter how extravagant it may be—it was not wired for the 1990s. We can barely imagine next week.

The technologies of the new century will often delight us and sometimes shock us. If we do not pursue them aggressively and dominate the relevant fields, they may also destroy us.

The Techno-Threat

In the year of our Lord 1999, it is fashionable to warn of the technological threat to the United States. In articles and at conferences, strategic thinkers warn of cyberattacks and physical terrorism that will wreck our vital infrastructure. The threats described are sometimes convincing and often worthy of consideration. But the apostles of insidious foreign genius always miss the salient point—we in the United States are the technologically empowered. Threat analysts warn us of our vulnerabilities yet overlook our strengths. They would have us spend as many billions as we can squeeze out of Congress on digital defense. They are the crippled children of the Cold War.

When it comes to defending our technological and communications infrastructure, we should bluntly put the burden on those in the private sector. They would be the biggest losers under the conditions of cyberattack—and they are also the best equipped to develop practical, affordable safeguards. Assigning our government the mission of defending every last computer terminal within our physical borders would prove both prohibitively expensive and ineffectual. Our government needs to regulate—lightly—in the information age, not undertake hopeless missions.

We do, of course, have a national defense requirement to protect the integrity of our information and infrastructure. The point is that we can only address those needs cooperatively, with the genius of the private sector developing its own defenses as it globalizes, while the U.S. armed forces, along with other relevant agencies, prepare offensive measures—the best defense is a good technological offense.

Instead of worrying about the ideal shape of a digital shield, we need to build cyberswords. We need to learn to patrol the digital lines of communications on which our prosperity depends. Instead of waiting to be attacked, we must develop a doctrine of preemptive information strikes. Our Special Operations Command should have a Cyber-Commando Force, recruited and retained with salary supplements such as we pay doctors and lawyers, that "deploys" into the dark shadows of the world's digital networks.

Eventually, we will need to evolve our information assault structures into a force that breaks down traditional boundaries between departments (those boundaries are slowly collapsing, in any case) to include Treasury officers, Commerce officials, communications experts, and those responsible for international law enforcement. Special Operations Cyber-Command could be the first true interdepartmental organization for the next century, and such an organization might prove crucial to our national integrity in the future. The fundamental requirement will not be money (although that will certainly be necessary) but a fresh appreciation of the inadequacy of present international law to address evolving threats. There is no real legal or moral requirement to grant foreigners the same rights and protections as we do our own citizens. To do so is pompous stupidity that endangers our own citizens while preventing us from helping the foreign victims of dictators, criminals, and terrorists.

We are a giant afraid of mice. Our technological strength should be the grounds for an energetic offensive approach to cyberattack, rather than a source of fears. We face asymmetrical threats—let us turn those asymmetries to our advantage. We must regain a sense of who we are and pride in what we are about. We *do* have a right to act abroad, whether in cyberspace or on foreign soil, if it benefits our citizens and the global rule of law.

Inevitable Weapons

The greatest opportunity for us, and the greatest danger to us, will come with the development of behavior-control weapons by the middle decades of the next century, if not sooner. On the one hand, these will be the weapons most horrible to our civilization, but we will be unable to prevent their development. In their perfected form, they will permanently alter the perceptions and beliefs of men and women. Depending on the technological forms they take, defending against them may prove to be the greatest challenge we have ever faced. On the other hand, they offer the first opportunity in history to pacify humankind without violence. In the first half of the next century, postmodern weapons may allow us to "outlaw" war. In subsequent decades, behavior-control mechanisms finally may let us stop genocide, oppression, fanaticism, and even criminality.

At the primitive level, a bullet is a very good behavior-control weapon. Properly employed, it permanently halts the misbehavior of the individual. But this discussion is about a more rarefied—and ultimately more frightening—level of manipulation. We—or our enemies, should we fail to act—*will* develop behavior-control weapons that change the mind without invading the body. In a sense, we already possess them today. A device as primitive as a car radio "controls" our behavior. We are more apt to get a speeding ticket while listening to a rock station than to a classical broadcast. Advertisers certainly perceive television as a behavior-control weapon. Hollywood movies jar the world with their thrills, temptations, and implicit messages of our cultural superiority (unfortunately concentrating on the material and sensual, when our real power is intellectual, creative-generative, and moral).

Imagine a weapon, directed at an individual or a mass, that compacts a lifetime's worth of carefully tailored signals into a microsecond broadcast. Imagine another weapon that targets specific nodes, or simply processes, in the brain. The insidious feature of such weapons is that the victim not only doesn't know what hit him but doesn't realize he has been hit by anything at all. He simply loses the desire to fight, suddenly regarding us amiably and cooperatively.

The dark side is that such weapons could permanently alter the perceptions of individuals and entire cultures. In the hands of a dictator or mass marketer, they would be monstrous (and civil libertarians will find them monstrous in any case, arguing that it is more humane to kill an individual than to interfere with his or her free will). Were we able to control the future fully, we might decline to develop them. But these weapons are coming with certainty. If there is any technology that we must first master and then prohibit elsewhere, it is the means to alter human thought. Otherwise, Armageddon may arrive not with a rain of fire but with a quiet suggestion.

Such weapons are theoretically ideal and practically logical, though a future historian looking back on this essay will no doubt laugh at the naiveté and crudity with which I have envisioned them. Given current developments in fields as diverse as neurobiology, anthropology, sonics, communications, digital engineeering, marketing, and complexity studies, the weapon I can envision most easily is some form of broadcast device. But I am as limited as the screenwriters of *Goldfinger* in my ability to imagine the future. The only thing of which I am certain is that the next century's revolution in weaponry will involve forms of behavior control and mental intrusion. Attacking the human body has been a sloppy and inefficient means of making war. Attacking the mind may prove the culmination of military history.

> *Attacking the human body has been a sloppy and inefficient means of making war. Attacking the mind may prove the culmination of military history.*

Our ability to "read" other human beings and respond to delinquent intent will develop in other forms before the advent of full-fledged behavior-control weapons. In the next few decades, customs inspectors will be able to detect smugglers through scent profiles, and infantrymen will be able to meter hostile intent as they fight through urban jungles. While one great breakthrough may change the military paradigm, it is more likely that these weapons will creep up on us incrementally. Either way, if we are not firmly the masters of the developmental process, we may face the ultimate Pearl Harbor.

The American Choice

This is our choice: Shall we dominate the earth for the good of humankind? Or will we risk the enslavement of our country and our civilization? Will we pursue asymmetrical weapons that allow us to eliminate the threat of weapons of mass destruction where that threat originates, in the human mind and soul? Or will we continue to insist that diplomatic niceties and the social prejudices of global elites demand that we wait, decade after decade, for evil men to act first? Will we protect our own citizens? Or will we continue to defend the rights of monsters?

If we are willing to fight for the future, to act in confidence and justice, we may create something akin to a golden age—so long the stuff of myth—for humanity. We will never be able to prevent every violent act, but we may be able to eliminate traditional wars, mass violence, and the use of weapons of mass destruction, including behavior-control weapons in renegade hands. If we have courage, we can serve mankind. If we prove cowards, the future may make the dying twentieth century look like paradise.